EAT KOREAN

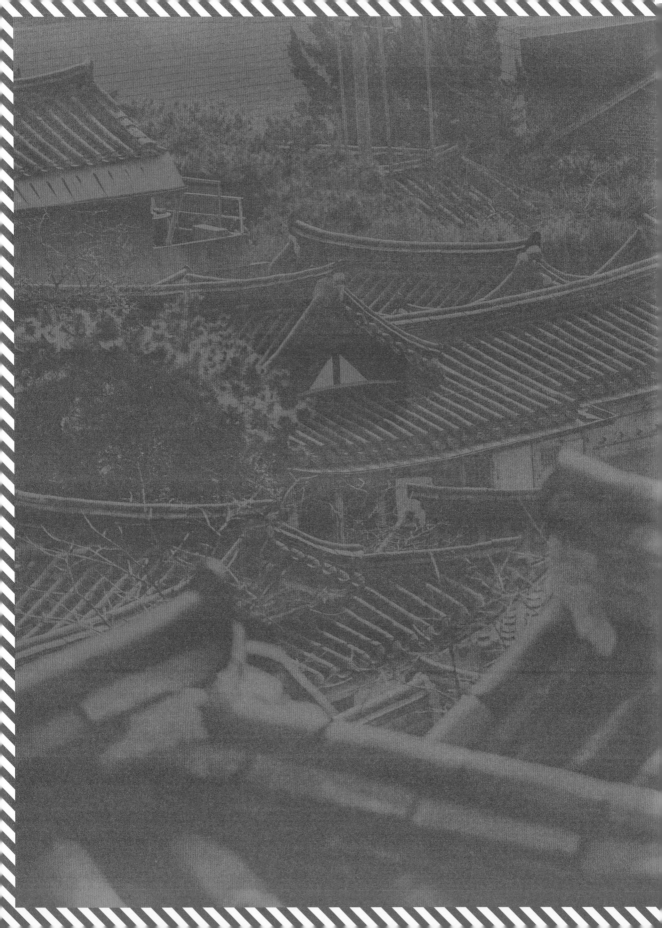

DA-HAE WEST

EAT KOREAN

our home cooking & street food

MITCHELL BEAZLEY

CONTENTS

YOU HAVE TO

measure it

TO KNOW IF IT'S

TOO LONG OR

too short

긴 짧은

Mostly about my mum...

I was born in Busan, South Korea but moved to England when I was three. Raised by my Korean mum and English dad, I couldn't really speak much English when we first moved here. When my mum dropped me off at nursery school for the first time, she worried about how I'd interact with the other kids with the language barrier – fortunately, kids are kids and just get on with it, creating strong bonds over toys, biscuits and nap times – so things actually turned out pretty well and language was never an issue.

It was incredibly important to my mum that I knew about the country that I came from, and I think this is why I was so proud of being Korean when I first started school. I'd write my name in scrawly Korean on top of all my school work (it was even mentioned in one of my school reports), and I'd always be the first to point out where Korea was on the world map.

My dad travelled away a lot for work, so whenever it was just my mum and I at home, we'd have Korean food for breakfast, lunch and dinner. Having eaten rice and *kimchi* for every meal since she was young, it was initially difficult for my mum to adapt to Western foods. Every time we visited Korea, she'd make sure to bring back enough bags of dried anchovies and *gochugaru* (Korean red chilli powder) in her suitcase to last us until our next trip. It was difficult to get Korean ingredients in the UK back then, so my resourceful mum would adapt recipes so that she could use the ingredients she could get hold of, along with the ones she'd snuck back in her suitcase. *Kkakdugi*, a Korean radish *kimchi* was made with swede or turnips in our house, *gochujang* (Korean red chilli paste) was homemade (there are photos of a three to four-year-old me, licking it off my hands and elbows), and my mum would also forage for the tips of wild fern (often eaten in *bibimbap*) and young rapeseed leaves to make her summer *kimchis*. Gradually, my mum took a little more interest in cooking other foods and, bit by bit, she learnt more about different non-Korean ingredients. Soon enough, Korean food became just one of many types of cuisine we enjoyed at home (much to my dad's relief).

While I was growing up in the UK, Korea went through some really tough economic times and was hit hard by the IMF crisis. Things looked pretty bleak for the country, but my mum would be insistent that one day Korea would become this great big economy that other countries would aspire to be. She'd try and push the importance of learning Korean, but going through my trickier teenage years, I took little interest in my lessons. They felt like a waste of time because, back then, it looked like Korea was always going to be this small, hidden country that no one knew anything about – at least to me.

Despite my disregard for my Korean lessons, I did look forward to our trips to Korea, and I was lucky enough to visit pretty often as I was growing up. Visits were packed full of rushing around to visit relatives, eating lots and revisiting my mum's childhood haunts, but in hindsight, it was the everyday things I loved most. Going to the market with my mum – so different to the markets in the UK and filled with such sights, sounds, smells and hustle and bustle. Going to the beach with my cousins. Going fishing. Swimming in the bath houses... I'm so thankful to have so many childhood memories there.

There was one particular holiday though that really cemented Korea as a second home for me. It was during one summer holiday while I was at university, and I went (slightly under duress at the time) to spend a few months living with my cousin Jisoo on Jeju Island. Jeju Island is the honeymoon destination of Korea and for good reason – a volcanic island full of mountains,

surrounded by crystal blue seas and with its own sunny microclimate that's warmer than the rest of Korea. It's impossible not to fall in love with it. I grew a whole new appreciation of Korea that I'd never had before. That summer was one of the best holidays I've ever had. Jisoo and I had such fun swimming, watching Korean dramas, ordering takeaway and eating Baskin Robbins until late into the night. It was the longest time I'd ever spent in Korea since moving to the UK, and I loved it.

Ever since that summer in Jeju, I started to take a lot more interest in Korea. I started speaking to my mum in Korean (she had persistently never given up trying) and I started to seek out more and more information about the country, and particularly the food. As I've grown up, I've seen Korea go from strength to strength and I couldn't help but sit up and take notice when Korean food and flavours started to creep onto small segments on TV and appear in fancy restaurant menus. Somewhere in the back of my mind, I wanted to be part of this – to link back to my Korean roots and promote the food I loved; I just didn't know how or where to start.

IT ALL STARTED WITH A MCDONALDS...

Gareth and I met through mutual friends in my last year of university and one of the reasons we got on so well from the beginning was because of our shared love of food. Gareth has always loved food. All food really. When he was growing up, he never really watched children's TV and instead was always fixated on cookery shows. He loved cooking and probably would have made a great chef (I think), but he'd never thought of doing it as a career. Instead, one of his first jobs was working at a pub and from there he worked his way up through hospitality until he reached the head offices of the restaurant group D&D London.

We got married in 2012 and went to Korea on our honeymoon. We'd spent several days with my family feasting on huge Korean dinners, with Gareth proclaiming that everything he ate was his new favourite dish. It was his first time in Korea and he hadn't known what to expect, but he was completely blown away by it all – and particularly the food.

In the past, it had always been difficult to try any sort of non-Korean food in Korea. Korea is full of really great Korean restaurants (most of which specialize in just one dish) but had resisted much culinary influence from other countries. Despite this, for as long as I can remember, it's always been possible to get a *bulgogi* burger at any one of the fast food restaurants. One night, we were walking from my aunt's house to our nearby hotel, when we wandered past a McDonalds. Like most global fast-food chains, McDonald's adapts their menu to the country that they're in, and in Korea, they have a *bulgogi* burger. It's a standard

McDonald's beef burger that's marinaded in a sweet, sticky soy glaze based on the Korean BBQ marinade. I'd told Gareth about this Korean twist on their burgers, and he was insistent that we try one. It wasn't the best burger that Gareth had ever eaten (though it was the best McDonald's he'd had), but the idea of marrying those Korean flavours with Western-style food stuck in our heads.

When we came back to England, we decided to try making some *bulgogi* burgers at home. They turned out better than we'd ever imagined, with the sweet, salty *bulgogi* marinade teasing out the meaty flavours from the burgers. Gareth ended up eating three in one sitting. As we ate them, we kept saying that if someone sold them in the UK, they'd be a real hit. Then it struck us... why couldn't that be us?

The more we thought about starting a Korean burger business together, the more it made sense. After those first *bulgogi* burgers we made at home, we started putting some plans together, finding some fantastic suppliers and testing lots of new recipes. Eight months later we traded at our first market as Busan BBQ.

Since starting Busan BBQ, we've been back to Korea a few times and have seen how the food is really starting to change there. Though great Korean food can still be found everywhere you look, there's been a wave of fusion Korean restaurants that have opened, which take Korean flavours and mash them with different cuisines. A lot of Korean Americans have taken the foods that they've grown up with and brought them back to Korea, and young Koreans are excited by the change.

Similarly, when we started Busan BBQ, very few people had heard of Korean food. We'd offer *kimchi* on our burgers and would have to explain what it was to almost every customer. Now, we can go easily go through 20 kilos of it in a weekend, with customers asking for more. There's been an explosion of interest in Korean cooking and ingredients over the past year or so, and we're so proud to be part of that.

This book is a combination of the recipes I've grown up with, along with new recipes that we've thought up along the way. Some of the recipes might not be as authentic as you'd imagine, but then, what is authentic nowadays, anyway? This is Korean cooking as we know it – the kind of food that's often thrown together to create something delicious. This is the food we love and we hope you'll love it too.

Essential Korean Ingredients

Failure
IS THE
Mother
OF ALL
Success

Korean food is predominantly based on a handful of ingredients, the most common of which are the jang – products which have been made from fermented soybeans. The jang include what I think of as the 'holy trinity' of Korean cooking – gochujang, doenjang and ganjang. Most dishes will contain at least one of these three ingredients.

Gochujang [1]

Gochujang is Korean red chilli paste. Made from fermented soybean powder, sweet rice flour and dried Korean chillies, *gochujang* is sweet and spicy but has a real depth of flavour and an earthiness that's very unique.

Doenjang [2]

Often described as Korean miso, *doenjang* is a fermented soybean paste. Unlike miso, the paste is quite coarse, often containing whole beans, and the flavour is much saltier and punchier.

Ganjang [3 and 4]

Ganjang is soy sauce, and was originally a by-product of the *doenjang*-making process. Korean soy sauce is often slightly sweeter and more caramel-like in flavour than other soy sauces. There are lots of different varieties of soy sauce, but the main two that we use in Korean cooking are *jin ganjang* [3], a regular soy sauce used for braising dishes, dipping sauces and marinades and *guk ganjang* [4], a much paler, saltier soy sauce used in soups and to lightly flavour dishes such as *muchims* (see page 60).

KEY CUPBOARD INGREDIENTS

The *jangs* aside, there are a few other essentials that you'll need in your cupboard for Korean cooking. These include:

Gochugaru [5]

Gochugaru is often described as 'Korean chilli powder', 'Korean red pepper powder' or 'Korean red pepper flakes'. Made from ground, dried Korean chillies, *gochugaru* comes in two types – fine or coarse. The fine *gochugaru* is used to make *gochujang*, whereas the coarse version is for everyday kitchen use. Whenever we mention *gochugaru* in this book, we're referring to these coarser flakes. *Gochugaru* is spicy but the chillies have a subtle, smoky sweetness to them. It is usually used when more heat is needed in a dish, rather than adding more *gochujang*. This is because adding too much *gochujang* can make a dish taste too salty whereas *gochugaru* just brings a little bit more spice.

Rice [6]

Koreans usually eat short-grain white rice (sushi rice), which has a high starch content that makes it sticky and shiny. Though most Korean dishes are based on sharing, everyone usually gets their own individual bowl of rice. Korean rice needs to be sticky, fluffy and glossy, which can only achieved with the perfect ratio of water to rice (see page 26).

Roasted Sesame Oil [7]

It is really important to have a good-quality, roasted, 100 per cent pure (not blended) sesame oil as part of your Korean larder. The good ones are pricier but are much stronger in flavour, and a little goes a really long way. Buying a cheap, blended version is a false economy as you end up having to use a lot more. Roasted sesame oil is not usually used for frying, as it has a much lower burning point than cooking oils such as vegetable oil, and is instead used in dipping sauces and marinades or to finish dishes as it gives a creamy, nutty aroma.

Roasted Sesame Seeds [8]

Sesame seeds can be bought already roasted, or you can buy plain ones which you toast yourself in a dry pan at home. You can buy black or white sesame seeds, but we usually use the white ones. These give a nice nutty texture and also look great sprinkled over a dish as a garnish.

Apple Vinegar [9]

We really like using apple vinegar as it has a distinctively fresh apple-y flavour that is tart and a little sweet. If you can't get hold of apple vinegar, rice or cider vinegar also work as substitutes in any of the recipes where apple vinegar is used in this book.

Seaweed

There are lots of different types of seaweed and, quite confusingly, the same varieties are often sold under different names. The three that we use in this book are:

Gim (also known as 'nori' or 'sushi' seaweed) [10] These are square sheets of seaweed, usually used for sushi. Sometimes these sheets come seasoned with oil and salt. The seasoned seaweed is great cut into squares and eaten simply with rice, or cut into matchstick-thin strips as a garnish.

Miyuk (also known as '*wakame*') [11] These usually come dried in long, thin packets and are used for soup. A little goes a very long way – as you rehydrate this seaweed in water it'll double in volume and go from crispy black strands to slippery green ribbons.

Dashima (also known as '*kombu*' or '*kelp*') [12] These are dried, tough sheets of seaweed, usually used for stock, which can be bought in long sheets or ready-cut. I usually use the ready cut-kind for ease. They often have a little bit of a white dusty coating on them – don't wash this off, as this is where all the flavour is.

Noodles

Noodles form an important part of the Korean diet, and come in a variety of different types, from thin vermicelli noodles made from flour, to springy buckwheat noodles, cellophane noodles made from sweet potato and last (but by no means least) the instant noodles, or *ramyun*, loved by all. For a detailed breakdown of noodle types, see page 162.

OTHER COMMON INGREDIENTS

In this book, you'll notice a few other ingredients that frequently pop up. These include:

Cabbage *Kimchi* [13]

As well as appearing as a side dish or *banchan* with almost every Korean meal, *kimchi* (see page 30) is often used for cooking. Cabbage *kimchi* is the most frequently used *kimchi* for cooking – it has to be matured for at least a few weeks so that the flavours have deepened and intensified and the *kimchi* is tangy and strong.

Sweet Rice Flour [14]

Also known as glutinous rice flour, *chapssal garu*, or more commonly *mochiko*, sweet rice flour is used in the fermentation process of both *gochujang* and *kimchi* and is also commonly used as a thickener for sauces and in batters (such as for our Korean Fried Chicken, see page 212).

Dried Anchovies [15]

Usually found in the frozen section of Korean and Asian supermarkets, dried anchovies come in lots of different sizes. The two we've used in this book are the tiny anchovies (which are no bigger than a fingernail) for frying as a *banchan* (see page 44) and the large dried anchovies, which form a key ingredient in our stock recipe (see page 22).

Fermented Shrimp [16]

These teeny, tiny shrimp or *saeujeot* are preserved through salting and can be found in jars and in the frozen section of Korean and Asian supermarkets. A common ingredient in *kimchi*, they make a great seasoning. A word of warning – as they're very salty, a little goes a long way!

Fish Sauce [17]

Fish sauce is a key ingredient in *kimchi*. It smells very pungent and fishy if you're not used to it, but this mellows as you cook with it (or in the case of *kimchi*, once the dish has fermented and matured).

14

16

15

17

13

20

18

21

19

Mandu Skins

Mandu skins are traditionally used to wrap a variety of savoury fillings and are then pan-fried, steamed, deep-fried or added to soups. While knowing how to make these dumpling wrappers is no means essential (they're so easy to find at any Chinese supermarket), you will get far more satisfaction from making your own (see page 24).

Mooli [18]

Though traditional Korean cooking would use Korean radishes, mooli are much easier to get hold of outside of Korea and taste quite similar. Mooli (also known as 'white radish' or 'daikon') are a long white vegetable that can be found in most Asian grocery stores. They are much milder in flavour than the peppery red English breakfast radishes and add a great crunch and texture to salads and slaws, but are also used in soups for body and for their clean, refreshing flavour.

Spring Onions [19]

Spring onions have been part of Korean cooking since long before the onion was introduced. They have a subtler flavour than normal onions and we often use the finely chopped green as a garnish.

Garlic and Ginger [20 and 21]

These two ingredients are as important as each other in Korean cooking, and are probably the ingredients that we've used the most in this book. Korean cooking is often quite punchy, so garlic and ginger are usually minced or very finely chopped for maximum flavour.

Korean/Asian pear

Unlike the European pears we're used to seeing, Korean pears are large and round, with a thick papery golden skin. The skin is usually peeled and discarded, and the fruit inside is very crisp, sweet and juicy. My favourite way to eat these are straight from the fridge, so that they're really cold and refreshing.

Yuja/Yuzu

Yuja (more commonly known as *Yuzu*) is a tangy citrus fruit with a slightly bitter edge, a bit like a grapefruit. As a fresh fruit, it resembles a mandarin but it's easier to get hold of as a concentrate (usually in small 70ml/2¼fl oz bottles). *Yuja* has a lovely fresh scent and makes a delicious alternative to lemons.

Jujube

Also known as *daechu* in Korean, *jujube* are small, red dried dates which have a sweet, earthy flavour and can be used in either desserts or savoury dishes. In Korea, they're known for their medicinal properties and are often sliced thinly to add to teas or used for cooking in dishes such as *sam gye tang*.

HOMEMADE STOCKS AND DIPPING SAUCES

There are a few base stock and dipping sauces recipes that you'll need to have up your sleeve. As you make your way through this book, you'll notice that you're constantly referred back to this section as they provide the backbone of a lot of Korean recipes.

Stocks

One of the most important basics stocks is *Myeulchi Gookmul* (see page 22), a mild, but deeply flavoured stock made from dried anchovies and kelp that provides the base for most Korean soups and stews. I do have a bit of a cheat's confession though – there are times when I don't always have dried anchovies at home, or I'm tired and don't want to bother with boiling up a new batch of stock. In these instances I use a light chicken or vegetable stock instead.

For the dishes that need big, meatier flavours, we've also included a recipe for a rich brown chicken stock (*Dak Yuksu*, see page 23), which is the perfect way to use up any carcasses from a leftover roast chicken and is packed full of flavour.

Dipping Sauces

There are a lot of overlaps when it comes to dipping sauces. Fried Korean dishes (of which there are many) can be quite heavy, so need something tangy such as our soy vinegar dipping sauce (*Cho Ganjang*, see page 21) to cut through the grease. Alternatively, some dishes just need a sauce so that everyone can season to their own taste, which is where our soy seasoning sauce (*Yangnyum Jang*, see page 21) comes in.

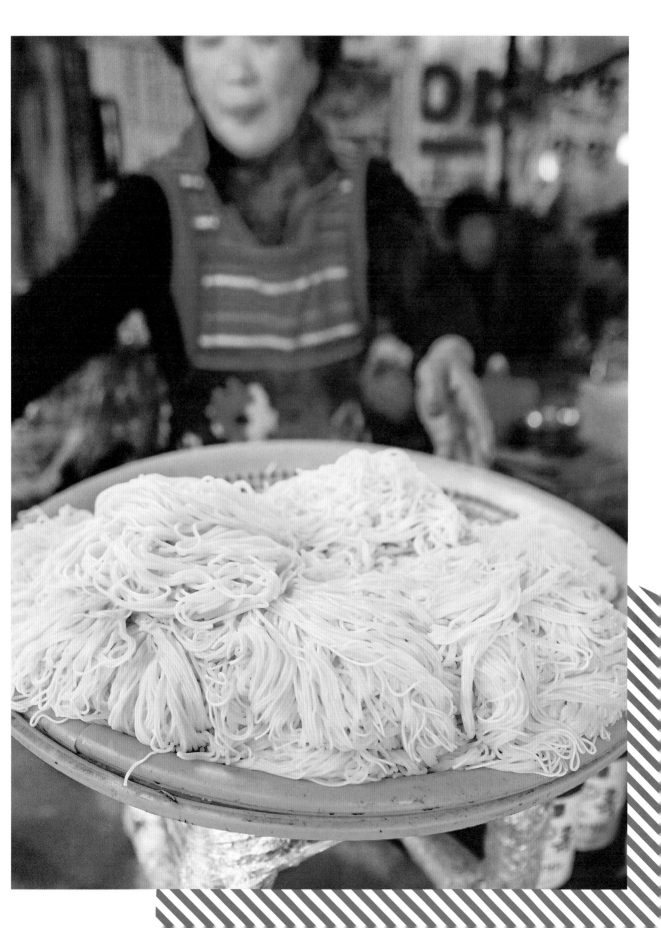

Cho Gochujang TANGY CHILLI DIPPING SAUCE

Translating as 'vinegared chilli paste', *cho gochujang* is sweet and spicy with a tart edge. In Korea it is usually eaten as a dipping sauce for raw fish known as *hwe* and is also often used as an ingredient in *banchan* sharing dishes such as *miyuk cho muchim* (see page 61).

SERVES
4

3 tablespoons *gochujang* (Korean red chilli paste)
1 tablespoon lemon juice
2 tablespoons apple vinegar

1 tablespoon caster sugar
2 garlic cloves, minced

Mix all the ingredients together in a bowl until well combined, then serve in individual dipping bowls.

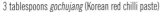

Supermarket Gochujang

Packed with salty, sweet umami flavour, *gochujang* brings both a unique heat and depth to anything you add it to, and is such an essential part of Korean cooking that other chilli sauces and pastes such as *sriracha* and *tobanjan* just don't make very good substitutes. While we're lucky to live close to a number of Korean supermarkets, when we started putting this book together it was really important for us to create an easy-to-make *gochujang* from ingredients that you could get hold of in a good ordinary supermarket, as we know that not everyone has this luxury. This really does taste similar to the real thing, so make a batch and leave it in your refrigerator so that you have it to hand!

MAKES
1
SMALL JAR

8 tablespoons white miso paste
4 tablespoons corn syrup
4 tablespoons cayenne pepper

2 tablespoons mirin
1 tablespoon caster sugar
1 garlic clove, minced

Mix all the ingredients together in a bowl until well combined. Decant into a sterilized jar and store in the refrigerator. It should keep for at least a month.

> **TIP:** This *gochujang* has a bit more of a fiery kick than the traditional variety, so if you're using it for cooking, reduce the quantities of the sauce slightly from what we've suggested (unless you like it hot, that is).

CHO GOCHUJANG

SSAMJANG

Ssamjang KOREAN BBQ DIPPING SAUCE

The 'ssam' in ssamjang refers to the lettuce wraps used for Korean BBQ, which is what this sauce is usually eaten with. It's a mixture of *gochujang* and *doenjang*, so it's quite earthy, a little salty and has a tiny bit of chilli to it, making it perfect with barbecued meats. *Ssamjang* is also often eaten in Korea as a dipping sauce for raw vegetables, as well as forming the base sauce for our *Ssamjang Mayo* (see page 83).

1 tablespoon *doenjang* (Korean soybean paste)
1 tablespoon *gochujang* (Korean red chilli paste)

½ spring onion, trimmed and finely chopped
2 garlic cloves, minced

1 teaspoon sesame oil
1 teaspoon sesame seeds

Put all the Ingredients In a bowl and mix together well, then serve in individual dipping bowls.

Yangnyum Jang SOY SEASONING SAUCE

With its salty, slightly spicy kick, this sauce can be found in every noodle house in Korea.

6 tablespoons regular soy sauce
1 tablespoon fish sauce
2 spring onions, trimmed and finely chopped

2 bird's eye chillies, trimmed and finely chopped
2 tablespoons *gochugaru* (Korean red chilli powder)
1 tablespoon water

1 teaspoon caster sugar
2 garlic cloves, minced

Mix all the ingredients together in a small serving bowl until well combined. Transfer to the middle of the table and serve with a bowl of *Kalguksu* (see page 173) or some simply steamed tofu.

Cho Ganjang SOY VINEGAR DIPPING SAUCE

Cho ganjang literally translates as 'vinegared soy sauce', with 'cho' referring to 'vinegar' and 'ganjang' the Korean word for 'soy sauce'. It's amazing how a little bit of vinegar can transform this sauce — it lightens it and gives it a really nice tanginess which works really well with fried dishes such as *Haemul Pajeon* (see page 54) or with simple dumplings such as *Gogi Mandu* (see page 53).

4 tablespoons dark soy sauce
2 tablespoons apple vinegar
4 teaspoons *gochugaru* (Korean red chilli powder)

Put all the ingredients in a bowl and mix together well, then serve in individual dipping bowls.

Myeulchi Gookmul ANCHOVY STOCK

Knowing how to prepare your own anchovy stock is a basic essential when it comes to Korean cooking, and it's so easy to make. It doesn't taste overly fishy as the anchovies are just dried and not salted, but it gives a really clean, deep savoury flavour to the many soups and stews in which it's used.

MAKES ABOUT **1.5l** *(2½ PINTS)*

375g (13oz) mooli, cut into 5-cm (2-inch) pieces
1 onion, roughly chopped
2 spring onions, trimmed and roughly chopped
4 whole garlic cloves

2 litres (3½ pints) water
15 large dried anchovies, halved and gutted
5 x 5-cm (2-inch) *dashima* (*kombu*) kelp squares

1_ Put the mooli, onion, spring onions, garlic cloves and 1 litre (1¾ pints) of the measurement water in a large saucepan or stockpot. Bring to the boil, then reduce the heat and continue to simmer for 20 minutes.

2_ Add the anchovies to the pot along with the kelp squares and the remaining water, return to the boil and cook for a further 20 minutes, skimming off and discarding any foam from the top of the stock with a slotted spoon as you go, until the liquid is a light brown. Remove from the heat and leave to cool.

3_ Once cool, strain the stock through a colander to remove the vegetables. Use straightaway or pour into a suitable container and refrigerate for up to two days, or freeze for longer.

Dak Yuksu RICH BROWN CHICKEN STOCK

> While most Korean soups and stews are traditionally made using the anchovy stock *Myeulchi Gookmul* (see opposite) as a base, I actually think this brown chicken stock works just as well as it's so rich and full of flavour. If you've had a roast chicken dinner this is a great way to use the leftovers, while if you're using a whole chicken, remove the breasts and set them aside for another day, as you won't need the extra meat in this recipe.

MAKES ABOUT
1l
(1¾ PINTS)

1kg (2lb 4oz) chicken wings
1 x 1.2kg (2lb 12oz) chicken, breasts removed or the
   leftover carcass from a roasted chicken
3 tablespoons vegetable oil, plus extra for greasing

2 large onions, roughly sliced
pinch of salt
4 whole garlic cloves
200g mooli, cut into 5-cm (2-inch) pieces

1_ Preheat the oven to 220ºC (425ºF), Gas Mark 7.

2_ Use the heel of a large knife to carefully press down on the chicken wings, cracking the bones. Repeat with the spine of the carcass and the chicken legs.

3_ Place the bones on a large greased roasting tray, spoon over 2 tablespoons of the vegetable oil and coat evenly. Roast for 45 minutes. Remove from the oven, skim off any fat that may have rendered down with a spoon and set aside.

4_ Heat the remaining 1 tablespoon of oil in a large, heavy-based saucepan or stockpot. Add the onions and salt and cook gently over a low heat, stirring occasionally, for 15 minutes or until the onions are golden brown and sticky.

5_ Add the garlic, mooli and chicken bones to the pot along with any sticky bits left on the bottom of the tray (these will be packed full of flavour). Pour over enough water to cover everything by about 2.5cm (1 inch) and bring to the boil. Lower the heat and simmer gently for 2 hours, skimming away any foam or fat deposits that collect on the top with a slotted spoon and topping up with extra cold water if the liquid gets below the level of the ingredients.

6_ Strain the solids from the liquid using a fine-mesh strainer or muslin and leave the stock to cool for at least 20 minutes, then scrape away any fat that may have collected on the top. Use straightaway or freeze in a suitable container for later.

Homemade Mandu (Dumpling) Skins

Although dumpling skins are easy to get hold of at any Chinese supermarket — and if you can't find them you can always use wonton or gyoza wrappers instead — it's really simple and satisfying to make your own. Homemade skins are more pliable so you can fill them with more filling and because they aren't so delicate, they're also more suitable for clumsy hands.

MAKES
22-24
DUMPLING SKINS

120g (4oz) plain flour, plus extra for dusting
pinch of salt
60ml (2fl oz) warm water, plus extra if needed

1_ Sift the flour into a large bowl, add the salt and mix together. Stir in the warm water a little at a time, mixing with a wooden spoon, until the mixture starts to come together to form a dough (you may need to add an extra teaspoon or two of water).

2_ Turn the dough out onto a lightly floured surface and knead for 10 minutes, then wrap in clingfilm and leave to rest in the refrigerator for 20 minutes.

3_ Once it has rested, knead the dough for a further 10 minutes until smooth and elastic.

4_ Shape the dough into a ball, then roll it out to a 2mm (¹/₁₆-inch) thickness. Cut out a circle using an 8-cm (3¼-inch) cookie cutter and leave the excess to one side. Repeat with the remaining dough pieces, lightly dusting each dough circle with a pinch of flour and covering loosely with clingfilm as you go. Gather together the excess dough, shape into a ball and roll out to make more dumpling skins.

5_ Fill the dumpling skins with sweet or savoury fillings and cook as per your chosen recipe, or freeze them to use later (see Tip).

TIP: *Mandu* freeze really well and are great for making up in big batches; just be sure that you lay them spaced out on a baking tray lined with clingfilm for their initial freezing so that they don't stick to each other. Once frozen they can be stacked. *Mandu* don't need to be defrosted before cooking – you just need to cook them for a little longer to make sure the filling is cooked through and the skins are browned.

How to Cook Rice the Korean Way

Cooking rice is actually a lot easier than most people think. This way of measuring the water vs. rice ratio will work for rice cookers, pressure cookers and saucepans. This is the way that most Koreans cook their rice, so here's the secret:

1_ Put 80g (2¾oz) uncooked short-grain rice per person into a large saucepan, making sure the rice sufficiently covers the bottom of your saucepan (so this works better for a minimum of 2 people). Fill the pan with enough water until covered. Rub the rice between your fingers in the water to wash off the excess starch, then pour the water away. Repeat at least twice more until the water runs clear.

2_ Smooth out the rice so that the surface is even, then lay your hand flat on top of the rice.

3_ Leaving your hand flat against the rice, fill the pan with water, until the water level reaches your knuckle (this will be about 2cm or ¾ inch above the rice).

4_ Place the saucepan over a high heat, cover with a lid and cook for 8 minutes, then reduce the heat to low and cook for a further 2 minutes.

5_ Turn the heat off and leave the saucepan with the lid on for a further 10 minutes – try to resist sneaking a peak at this stage as you don't want to release the steam from the pan.

6_ Once the rice has finished steaming, use a plastic rice spoon to separate the rice grains so that the rice is nice and fluffy.

TIP: If you have an electric hob, this method might need a little tweaking and playing around with as the hobs hold their heat. When you reach step 5, move the pan onto a cold hob so that the residual heat doesn't scorch the bottom of the pan.

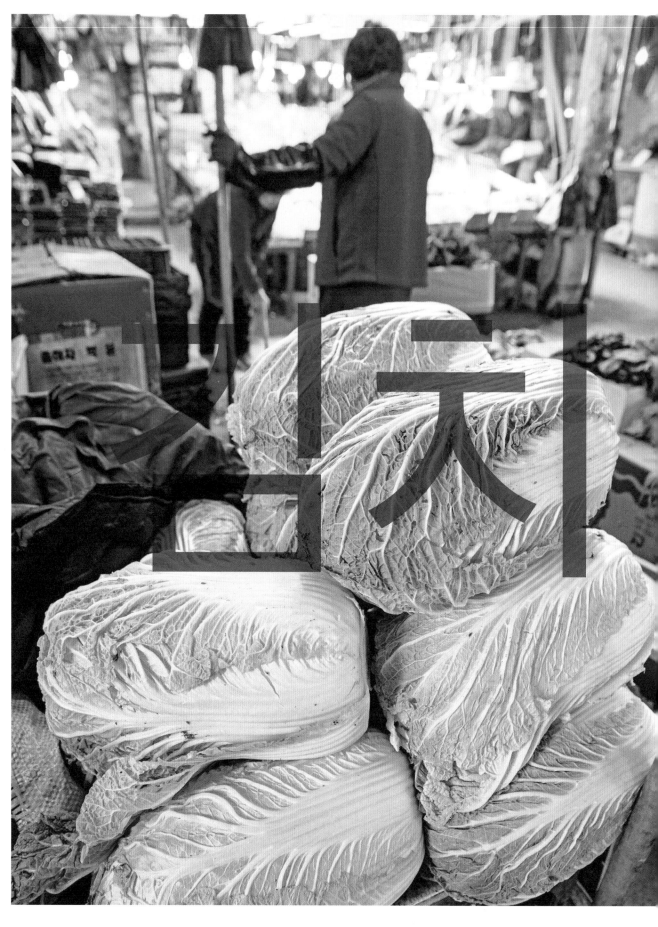

Kimchi

02

EVEN THE
Monkey
FALLS
FROM THE
TREE

You can't have a Korean meal without the country's favourite side dish, kimchi. An essential banchan or sharing dish, as well as an important ingredient in cooking, kimchi is so central to the Korean diet that it is eaten for breakfast, lunch and dinner. In fact, most Koreans even have a kimchi refrigerator in their apartment to store their kimchi at a cool temperature (and to avoid everything else in their refrigerator from taking on the strong kimchi flavours).

Traditionally a way of preserving vegetables for their nutrients in preparation for the long, harsh Korean winter, *kimchi* has been around in different guises as part of the Korean diet for centuries. When it was first made, vegetables were simply salted without any chilli (chilli didn't make its way to Korea until the 17th century), but since chilli was introduced, it quickly became an important ingredient in most *kimchis* and nowadays, *kimchi* is often associated with the bright red colour of the chilli pepper.

During the late autumn months, a lot of Koreans start a process called *Kimjang*, which is when families and neighbourhoods get together to create huge batches of *kimchi* to last them through the winter. For *Kimjang*, *Baechu Kimchi* (see page 32) or cabbage *kimchi* is usually made, which is the most common type of *kimchi* and the one used most for cooking – all the recipes that call for *kimchi* in this book refer back to this one. When cooking *kimchi*, it's really important that the *kimchi* is fermented for at least three weeks so that it's strong, pungent and full of flavour. If you cook with *kimchi* when it's too young, you're essentially just cooking with cabbage so the flavour easily washes away, which means your stews will be watery and lack flavour and your fried rice will have no spicy tang. *Kimchi* that has been fermented for several weeks (even months) is best for soups and stews.

Baechu kimchi can be quite strong and spicy but there are also a lot of other *kimchi* varieties. *Geotjeori* (see page 36) is a *kimchi* that's usually eaten in the spring and summer – it's light and fresh and can be enjoyed as a salad as a nice contrast to the strong *baechu kimchi* of the winter. Other types include *Dongchimi* (see page 40) – a water kimchi that doesn't contain any chilli flakes, so the liquid is clear and refreshing. As well as seasonal varieties, *kimchi* in Korea differs depending on the region that it's made in. *Kimchi* produced in the northern areas such as Seoul are often quite mild, whereas *kimchi* from the warm southern areas are often quite spicy, salty and contain a lot of fermented fish products due to their proximity to the coast. The *kimchi* recipes in this book are based on the *kimchi* that I've grown up with. My family is from Busan, so these *kimchi* are probably more strongly flavoured than those you might have tried before.

While it's pretty easy to buy *kimchi* nowadays, either online or from Asian supermarkets, the bought kind will always taste different to making your own, not to mention the sense of achievement you'll get from whipping up your own batch. It's possible to '*kimchi*' pretty much anything, and we wanted to demonstrate this in this book by including some more unusual *kimchi* varieties such as Mango *Kimchi* (see page 38) and Tomato *Kimchi* (see page 41). These *kimchis* are not traditional, but are examples of how the process can be used to ferment almost any firm vegetable or fruit that you might have lying around your refrigerator at home.

Baechu Kimchi EVERYDAY CABBAGE *KIMCHI*

When I was little, I used to watch my mum make *kimchi*. Stood over a sink, elbow-deep in the *kimchi* 'glue', she would rub the mixture into the cabbage before tearing off a bit of one of the spicy leaves to feed me. One bit was never enough, and I'd always sneak some more until she'd give in and we'd enjoy a pile of the newly made *kimchi* with a steaming bowl of rice. *Kimchi* at this stage is very different to what you might be familiar with — it's fresh and crisp, like a spicy salad, and is deliciously addictive in its own right. If you have the patience to give it a few weeks though, the *kimchi* will develop its characteristic tangy flavour through fermentation, and it is at this stage that it makes a great base for cooking with. No Korean meal is complete without it.

MAKES APPROX 800g (1LB 12OZ)

1 Chinese cabbage, about 800g (1lb 12oz), outer leaves and stem removed
50g (1¾oz) salt

KIMCHI 'GLUE'
150ml (¼ pint) *Myeulchi Gookmul* (see page 22)

1 tablespoon sweet rice flour
4 tablespoons *gochugaru* (Korean red chilli powder)
2 spring onions, trimmed and finely chopped
1 carrot, finely chopped
4 garlic cloves, minced

1-cm (½-inch) piece of fresh root ginger, peeled and very finely chopped
1 apple, finely chopped (skin on)
1½ tablespoons fish sauce
2 teaspoons *saeujeot* (salted fermented shrimp)

1_ Using a sharp knife, make a cut about 10cm (4 inches) up the cabbage to the base and use it to gently pull the cabbage in half (this helps to keep the leaves whole without shredding them). Repeat the process with each half so that the cabbage is quartered.

2_ Fill a large bowl with cold water and submerge each of the cabbage quarters fully, then remove from the water and shake them to get rid of any excess water. Take a small handful of salt and rub it up and down each leaf of 1 cabbage quarter, ensuring the thicker parts closer to the stalk are particularly well covered. Repeat with the remaining quarters, then transfer to a large, clean, clip lock plastic container and leave to brine for 3 hours, turning the cabbage quarters every 30 minutes to make sure the salt is distributed evenly over the cabbage.

3_ Meanwhile, make the *kimchi* 'glue'. Bring the stock to a boil in a small saucepan. Add the sweet rice flour, reduce the heat to a simmer and whisk together until there are no lumps and the mixture is thick enough to easily coat the back of a spoon. Set aside to cool to room temperature, then add the remaining 'glue' ingredients and mix together thoroughly (this is easiest done by hand, wearing gloves).

4_ After brining, thoroughly wash the cabbages under cold running water to remove any excess salt or sediment that that be trapped between the leaves, then shake dry. Take a small handful of the 'glue' and rub it up and down each leaf of 1 cabbage quarter to

coat, making sure that the thicker parts nearer the base are particularly well covered as before. Repeat with the remaining cabbage quarters.

5_ Fold over the top third of each cabbage quarter into its centre, then fold over the outer leaves to form a parcel. Pack the *kimchi* parcels tightly into the large container. Spoon any leftover 'glue' into the container to fill any gaps – this will help form a barrier against the air and prevent mould. Be sure to leave some space at the top of the container though, as the *kimchi* will need some room to ferment and expand (without it, you could end up with a *kimchi* explosion).

6_ Leave at room temperature for 3–4 days to ferment, then transfer to the refrigerator until needed. The *kimchi* will continue to ferment but at a much slower rate, so every day it'll taste a little sharper and a little tangier. Enjoy with everything.

TIP: One way I like to eat really fermented *kimchi* is to wash the leaves of their seasoning paste, then use these washed leaves to wrap barbecued meats, or simply lay the washed *kimchi* in one hand, put a small spoonful of rice in the middle with a dollop of *gochujang* and wrap it up to make a tasty little *kimchi* parcel.

Bok Choy and Radish Kimchi

This is the first non-traditional *kimchi* that Gareth and I ever made. The juicy, crunchy bok choy and radishes make it feel fresh, light and summery — quite different to the typical cabbage *kimchi*. I once gave a masterclass on how to make different types of *kimchi* and this was by far the most popular. I think people find it less intimidating as it doesn't have the same strong, fermented taste as the more traditional varieties. If you're a *kimchi* newbie, give it a try.

MAKES APPROX
1.5kg
(3LB 5OZ)

1kg (2lb 4oz) bok choy
250g (9oz) French radishes, trimmed and halved
1 tablespoon salt
1 tablespoon caster sugar

KIMCHI 'GLUE'
250ml (9fl oz) water
2 tablespoons sweet rice flour
2 tablespoons *gochugaru* (Korean red chilli powder)
2 spring onions, trimmed and finely chopped

1 carrot, grated
2 tablespoons *saeujeot* (salted fermented shrimp)
1 tablespoon fish sauce
6 garlic cloves, minced
2-cm (1-inch) piece of fresh root ginger, peeled and very finely chopped

1_ Using a sharp knife, make a cut about 5cm (2 inches) long to the base of each bok choy and use it to gently pull the bok choy in half (this helps to keep the leaves whole without shredding them). Repeat the process with each half so that the bok choy are quartered, then rinse the quarters along with the radishes under cold running water. Drain, shaking off any excess water, and set aside.

2_ To make the *kimchi* 'glue', bring the measurement water to a boil in a small saucepan. Reduce the heat to a simmer, add the sweet rice flour and whisk together until there are no lumps and the mixture is thick enough to easily coat the back of a spoon. Set aside to cool to room temperature, then add the remaining 'glue' ingredients and mix together thoroughly.

3_ Meanwhile, mix together the salt and sugar in a bowl. Add the bok choy quarters and rub the salt and sugar mixture between the leaves, ensuring the thicker parts near the base are particularly well covered. Transfer to a large, clean, clip lock plastic container along with the radish halves and mix everything together with your hands. Leave to brine for 30 minutes.

4_ After brining, thoroughly wash the bok choy and radishes under cold running water then shake dry. Take a small handful of the 'glue' and rub it up and down each bok choy quarter to coat, again making sure that the thicker parts nearer the base are particularly well covered. Use the leftover 'glue' to coat the radishes.

5_ Fold over the top third of each bok choy quarter into its centre, then fold over the outer leaves to form a parcel. Pile the folded bok choy parcels neatly back in the container, filling any gaps with the radish halves.

6_ This *kimchi* can be eaten straightaway, but is best after it has had 3–4 days at room temperature to ferment, after which you can store it in the refrigerator. It's not great for cooking, so if you want to make a *Kimchi Jjigae* (see page 138) or *Kimchi* Fried Rice (see page 164) you are better off using a traditional *Baechu Kimchi* (see page 32).

Geotjeori QUICK *KIMCHI* SALAD

After a long winter of eating strong fermented *baechu kimchi*, Koreans start to crave something lighter and fresher in spring. *Geotjeori* is a quick *kimchi* that's meant to be enjoyed the day you make it. Crunchy, sweet and eaten like a salad, it makes a great side dish to barbecued meats and fish.

MAKES APPROX 800g (1LB 12OZ)

1 Chinese cabbage, about 800g (1lb 12oz), outer leaves and stem removed
2 tablespoons salt
½ medium onion, finely sliced
1 spring onion, trimmed and finely sliced

3½ tablespoons *gochugaru* (Korean red chilli powder)
3 garlic cloves, minced
1-cm (½-inch) piece of fresh root ginger, peeled and very finely chopped
1 tablespoon fish sauce

2 tablespoons caster sugar
1½ tablespoons sesame seeds
cooked short-grain rice, to serve (see page 26)

1_ Using a sharp knife, make a cut about 5cm (2 inches) up the cabbage to the base and use it to gently pull the cabbage in half. Repeat the process with each half so that the cabbage is quartered, then repeat again so that the cabbage is split into eighths.

2_ Cut off and discard the tough base from the bottom of each cabbage section so that it breaks apart into separate leaves. Place the leaves in a large container and sprinkle over the salt, then mix together with your hands to ensure the leaves are completely coated. Leave to brine for 30 minutes, mixing every 10 minutes to ensure the salt is distributed evenly.

3_ After brining, thoroughly wash the cabbage leaves under cold running water to remove any excess salt, then drain, squeezing out any excess water, and place in a large bowl together with the remaining ingredients. Mix together with your hands thoroughly for 5 minutes, squeezing the leaves as you go – this will release water from the leaves and create a quick sauce. Serve immediately with bowls of rice.

TIP: While this *kimchi* is particularly good eaten the day you make it, you can leave it for a couple of weeks to ferment and enjoy its slightly sweeter flavour in your cooking in the same way as *Baechu Kimchi* (see page 32).

Kkakdugi CRUNCHY SWEDE *KIMCHI*

This super simple *kimchi* is one that my mum would often quickly throw together as I was growing up. *Kkakdugi* is traditionally made from cubed Korean radish (or moo), though back then swede and turnip were much easier to get hold of in the supermarket, and mum would often use these. Mooli, a very similar radish to moo, is easy to find these days in Asian grocery stores and makes a great alternative.

MAKES APPROX 1.2kg 2LB 11OZ

2 tablespoons salt
2 tablespoons caster sugar
1.2kg (2lb 12oz) swede, cut into 2.5-cm (1-inch) cubes

3-cm (1¼-inch) piece of fresh root ginger, peeled and very finely chopped
12 garlic cloves, minced

4 tablespoons *gochugaru* (Korean red chilli powder)
2 tablespoons fish sauce

1_ Mix together the salt and sugar in a large plastic sealable container. Add the swede cubes, toss to coat and set aside for 1 hour.

2_ After 1 hour, drain the liquid from the swede. Add the ginger, garlic, *gochugaru* and fish sauce. Mix everything together well.

3_ Leave the *kimchi* to ferment at room temperature for 1 week, testing every couple of days to check how strong it tastes, then transfer to the refrigerator and store until needed, when the strength has developed to suit your taste.

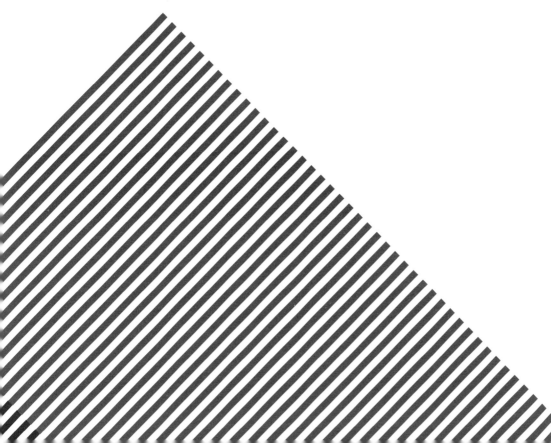

Mango Kimchi

While not an obviously Korean ingredient, mangoes really symbolize sunshine for me. I once spent a summer in Jeju Island where some of my family run a mango orchard, and while I was there I was lucky enough to eat the sweet, juicy fruit almost every day. This *kimchi* isn't as strange as it sounds, with the mango bringing a really lovely sweetness to the usually spicy *kimchi* ingredients. It's a great side for a summertime Korean BBQ and goes perfectly with our Pomegranate-glazed Lamb Kebabs (see page 120).

MAKES APPROX **500g** (1LB 2OZ)

3 x 300g (10½oz) unripe mangoes, peeled, stones removed and cut into 2.5-cm (1-inch) cubes
2 spring onions, trimmed and finely chopped
1 long red chilli, roughly chopped
3 tablespoons fish sauce

2 tablespoons *gochugaru* (Korean red chilli powder)
5-mm (¼-inch) piece of fresh root ginger, peeled and very finely chopped
2 garlic cloves, minced

1_ Put everything in a large, clean, clip lock plastic container and mix together well to ensure the mango cubes are evenly coated.

2_ Leave the *kimchi* to ferment at room temperature for 3 days before transferring to the refrigerator until needed.

Dongchimi REFRESHING WATER *KIMCHI*

Unlike most other *kimchi*, *dongchimi* doesn't contain any *gochugaru*, so is a lovely clear, white colour. While traditionally made as a winter *kimchi* (when the Korean radishes are in season), it's particularly delicious in summer and its refreshing, cool *kimchi* liquid is often used as a base for chilled noodle soups.

MAKES APPROX
800g
1LB 12OZ

2 tablespoons salt
2 tablespoons caster sugar
1 mooli, cut into 5-cm (2-inch) x 2-cm (¾-inch) batons
5-cm (2-inch) piece of fresh root ginger, peeled and
    thinly sliced

4 whole garlic cloves
1 apple, cut into finger-sized batons
2 spring onions, trimmed and cut into thirds
2 long red chillies, trimmed and cut into thirds
1 litre (1¾ pints) water

1_ Mix together the salt and sugar in a large, clean, clip lock plastic container. Add the mooli batons, toss to coat and set aside for 4 hours, mixing every 30 minutes to ensure the salt and sugar are distributed evenly.

2_ After 4 hours, add the remaining ingredients and mix everything together well. Leave the *kimchi* to ferment at room temperature for 2–3 days before transferring to the refrigerator until needed.

Tomato Kimchi

Because soft fruit and vegetables such as cucumbers take on *kimchi* flavours so well, Gareth had it stuck in his head that a tomato version would really work. It turns out he was right. This *kimchi* gets the best out of tomatoes that might not be quite as ripe as you want them to be by intensifying their natural sweetness.

MAKES
1kg
2LB 4OZ

½ tablespoon salt
½ tablespoon caster sugar
1kg (2lb 4oz) tomatoes, deseeded and cut into quarters

1½ tablespoons *gochugaru* (Korean red chilli powder)
1-cm (½-inch) piece of fresh root ginger, peeled and very finely chopped

3 garlic cloves, minced
1 tablespoon fish sauce
2 spring onions, trimmed and finely sliced

1_ Mix together the salt and sugar in a large, clean, clip lock plastic container. Add the tomato quarters, toss to coat and set aside for 30 minutes, mixing again every 10 minutes to ensure the salt and sugar are distributed evenly.

2_ Add the remaining ingredients to the container and, using your hands, mix them together until thoroughly combined.

3_ Leave the *kimchi* to ferment at room temperature for 3 days before transferring to the refrigerator until needed.

Banchan & Sides

03

IF YOU BRUSH

THEM OFF

YOU'LL FIND THAT

EVERYONE HAS

Some Dust

Food is so ingrained in Korean culture that the word for family, shikgu, translates literally as 'mouths to feed'. Every family gathering always involves a big feast and, whenever we meet with friends, the first thing we talk about is where we should eat.

While Korea's probably best known for its barbecued meats, these are usually reserved for eating out in big groups. At home, people tend to eat an assortment of small dishes known as *banchan* — meat, fish or vegetable dishes which are shared in the middle of the table, with each person also having an individual bowl of rice and often a simple soup, or *guk*, as well.

Banchan usually fall into the broad categories of *kimchi* (fermented vegetables), *namul* (lightly seasoned vegetable dishes), *bokkeum* (stir-fried dishes), *jorim* (braised dishes, usually in soy sauce) and *jeon*, which includes savoury pancakes (or *pajeon*) but also includes pan-fried meat or vegetables which are coated in a flour and egg batter. Because Koreans believe that balance is important in order to maintain a healthy diet, there will often be a real mix of different dishes served at any one time.

Nowadays, a lot of (particularly younger) Koreans don't have the time to make a variety of different *banchan* each day, but fortunately they're always easy to buy from the *ajummas* in the markets. Anyone who lives in Korea knows that it is run by the *ajummas* — the middle-aged women of Korea often seen wearing baggy floral trousers or shell suits and visors. They're the ladies with attitude — the ones who will push past you in a street or jump a queue without a second thought. But they're also the powerhouses. It's the *ajummas* who usually run the restaurants, cooking up a storm in the kitchen. They're also the ones with the big trays of food balanced on their heads as they run takeaways, and the ones that sit for hours at the markets, selling their veg and prepared *banchans*.

At work, I used to eat lunch with a group of girls, and we'd always each bring in at least one *banchan*, sometimes homemade, sometimes bought, for everyone to share. These would vary from the traditional such as homemade *kimchi* or seasoned vegetables to mac 'n' cheese, fried Spam or hot-dogs tossed in ketchup. It just goes to show that nowadays with *banchan* almost anything goes. It's what I love about Korean food in general — the fact that you're able to pick and choose the dishes you like to suit your own taste.

The dishes that we've included in this section are mostly traditional Korean *banchan*, but they can also be enjoyed as side dishes or starters. We've also included some of our favourite sides that we've served at our pop-ups and events, all of which would make equally great *banchan* too.

Jeon FAMILY FRITTERS

Though traditionally part of Korea's royal cusine, nowadays *jeon* can be found everywhere, even as street food. These lightly coated fritters still have a place, however, as part of special occasions, such as *Je-Sah* — when families get together to commemorate the lives of relatives who have passed away. In my family we hold a big *Je-Sah* gathering each year to commemorate my grandparents, and these *jeon* always form an important part of the meal we share.

SERVES
4–6

1 tablespoon vegetable oil, plus extra if needed
jeon pieces of your choice (see below)
Cho Ganjang (see page 21), to serve

COATING
4 eggs
160g (6oz) plain flour
1 teaspoon salt

1_ Heat the vegetable oil in a large heavy-based frying pan over a medium-low heat.

2_ To make the coating, whisk the eggs together in a bowl and set aside. In a separate bowl, mix together the flour and salt.

3_ Toss your chosen *jeon* pieces in the flour until well coated, then dip them in the beaten egg mixture.

4_ Shake off any excess beaten egg, then add the *jeon* pieces to the pan, being careful not to overcrowd it (you may need to cook these in batches, if so add an extra tablespoon of oil to the pan for each batch).

5_ Fry for 2–3 minutes on each side until golden brown, reducing the temperature if it looks like the *jeon* pieces are starting to colour too quickly. Remove from the pan and drain on kitchen paper. Serve with *cho ganjang* for dipping.

Cod (*sengsun*) *Jeon*
Cut 350g (12oz) cod fillet into 5-cm (2-inch) x 2.5-cm (1-inch) pieces. Coat and cook according to the instructions opposite.

Courgette (*hobak*) *Jeon*
Slice 1 courgette into 1-cm (½-inch) rounds. Coat and cook according to the instructions opposite.

Pork Meatball (*wanja*) *Jeon*
Crumble 200g (7oz) firm tofu into a large mixing bowl. Add 1 sliced spring onion, 4 finely chopped garlic cloves, 2 tablespoons diced carrot and 300g (10½oz) minced pork, season with salt and pepper and mix together well. Shape into golf-ball-sized pieces and flatten each until they are about 1cm (½ inch) thick. Coat and cook according to the instructions opposite.

Spring Onion and Spam *Jeon* Skewers (spam *sanjeok*)
Soak 8 bamboo skewers in water. Cut 8 spring onions into thirds, then slice 300g (10½oz) Spam into pieces of the same size as the onions. Alternately thread 3 spring onion and 3 Spam pieces onto each skewer, trim the skewer ends neatly, then coat and cook according to the instructions opposite.

HOBAK JEON

SENGSUN JEON

SPAM SANJEOK

Dubu Kimchi STIR-FRIED PORK AND *KIMCHI* WITH TOFU

Don't knock this until you've tried it! While *kimchi* and tofu might not sound like the most exciting of flavour combinations, it really works – the spicy tanginess of the *kimchi* contrasting with the soft, silky texture of the tofu. A great side dish, this is also often served as an *anju* as it makes a perfect accompaniment to a few shots of *soju*.

SERVES
4-6
AS A BANCHAN

1 tablespoon vegetable oil
300g (10½oz) pork belly, cut into bite-sized chunks
300g (10½oz) *Baechu Kimchi* (see page 32), drained and
   roughly chopped
1 tablespoon *gochugaru* (Korean red chilli powder)

1 tablespoon caster sugar
½ tablespoon roasted sesame seeds
½ tablespoon sesame oil
400g (14oz) firm tofu

1_ Heat the vegetable oil in a heavy-based frying pan over a medium heat. Add the pork and fry for 2–3 minutes, stirring, until the meat is coloured on all sides and cooked through.

2_ Add the *kimchi*, *gochugaru* and sugar to the pan and fry for another 3 minutes, until the *kimchi* softens and becomes glossy from the fat that has rendered down from the pork pieces. Add the sesame seeds and sesame oil and cook, stirring, for a further minute, then remove from the heat and set aside.

3_ Bring a saucepan of salted water to the boil. Carefully lower the tofu into the water, reduce to a simmer and cook for 3 minutes. Remove the tofu from the pan with a slotted spoon and drain on kitchen paper, then cut into 5-cm (2-inch) squares.

4_ Arrange the tofu squares on a serving plate or board and spoon over the pork and *kimchi* mixture to serve.

Gogi Mandu PORK DUMPLINGS

These plump little dumplings are always a real crowd pleaser. This recipe shows how to make the pan-fried versions with their crispy, golden brown skins, but they're also great simply steamed or added to soups, and can be deep-fried for added crunch too. I love adding them to instant noodles when I'm feeling really hungry.

MAKES
20
MANDU

vegetable oil, for frying
20 *mandu* skins, either shop-bought or homemade
  (see page 24)
2 tablespoons water, plus extra if needed
Cho Ganjang (see page 21), to serve

FILLING
3 dried shiitake mushrooms
50g (1¾oz) *dangmyeon* sweet potato noodles (see
  page 162)
200g (7oz) firm tofu
2 spring onions, trimmed and finely sliced
¼ Chinese cabbage, trimmed and finely sliced

3 garlic cloves, minced
pinch of pepper
2 tablespoons regular soy sauce
2 teaspoons sesame oil
1 tablespoon vegetable oil
300g (10½oz) minced pork

1_ For the filling, place the shiitake mushrooms in a bowl, cover with boiling water and leave to soak for 15 minutes. Drain and finely chop.

2_ Meanwhile, soak the noodles in boiling water in a separate bowl for 10 minutes. Drain and rinse under cold running water, then cut into 5-mm (¼-inch) lengths.

3_ Crumble the tofu into a large bowl (the finer you can crumble it, the better). Add the noodles and mushrooms to the tofu along with all the remaining filling ingredients except the minced pork and mix together well.

4_ Heat 1 tablespoon of vegetable oil in a frying pan over a medium heat. Add the minced pork, stirring, and break it into pieces with a wooden spoon until browned all over. Add the filling mixture into the pan and cook for a further 3 minutes, stirring, until the cabbage has softened. Tip the filling into a large bowl and leave to cool.

5_ Fill the *mandu* skins following the step-by-step instructions opposite.

6_ Heat 2 tablespoons of oil in a large frying pan with a lid over a medium heat. Add the *mandu*, being careful not to overcrowd the pan (you may need to do this in batches) and fry for 2 minutes until browned on one side.

7_ Turn the *mandu* over, add the water and cover with the lid. Cook for a further 2 minutes, then remove the

lid. The *mandu* should be half-crispy and half-steamed at this point – if there's still a little water in the pan, then leave them to cook uncovered for another minute until it has evaporated.

8_ Drain on kitchen paper and serve with *cho ganjang* for dipping.

MANDU-FILLING STEP-BY-STEP

1_ Lay a *mandu* skin flat in the palm of your hand.

2_ Spoon 2 teaspoons of the filling into the centre of the *mandu* skin.

3_ Dab a finger in a little water and run it over the edge of half of the *mandu* skin.

4_ Fold the *mandu* skin over and seal the edges together with your fingertips.

5_ Dab your finger in a little more water and run it over the front flat edge of the *mandu*.

6_ Ensuring the *mandu* skin remains flat, pinch the semicircular edge with your fingertips every 1-cm (½-inch) gap to create a rippled, crimped effect. Repeat with the remaining *mandu* skins and filling.

Haemul Pajeon CRISPY SEAFOOD PANCAKE

Apparently, Koreans traditionally eat these deliciously crispy savoury pancakes on rainy days because the sizzling noises from the frying pan sound like the pitter-patter of raindrops. While this seems like a bit of a stretch to me, I'm happy for any excuse! The baking powder is the secret ingredient in this recipe — it gives the pancake extra crunch, so everyone will be fighting over all those crispy edges. It's served traditionally with *makgeolli*, a fermented alcoholic rice drink, but it is also great with a *soju* or beer.

MAKES 2 LARGE PANCAKES

250g (9oz) plain flour
1 teaspoon salt
1 teaspoon baking powder
375ml (13fl oz) ice-cold sparkling water

200g (7oz) mixed seafood (such as prawns, mussels and squid rings), roughly chopped
2 bird's eye chillies, finely chopped (optional)
10 spring onions, trimmed and cut into

5-cm (2-inch) lengths
6 tablespoons vegetable oil, plus extra if needed
Cho Ganjang (see page 21), to serve

1_ In a large bowl, mix the flour, salt and baking powder together with the water to form a smooth batter. Add the seafood, chillies and spring onions and stir together well to ensure everything is evenly coated in the batter mixture.

2_ Heat 3 tablespoons of vegetable oil in a large, nonstick frying pan over a high heat. Spoon a generous ladleful of the pancake mixture into the centre of the pan then, using the base of the ladle, carefully smooth the mixture out into a circle shape until the pancake is about 1cm (½ inch) thick.

3_ Cook the pancake for 2–3 minutes, until browned and crispy on one side, then flip it over and cook for a further 2–3 minutes. The pancake will soak up some of the oil, so you may need to add a little extra to stop it sticking (this will also help to make the edges extra crispy!). Drain on kitchen paper and cover to keep warm.

4_ Heat the remaining 3 tablespoons of oil in the pan and repeat for the second pancake. Serve with *cho ganjang* for dipping.

Coconut Bindaetteok CRISPY MUNG BEAN PANCAKES

These mung bean pancakes are particularly famous in Gwangjang Market in Seoul. There you can watch as the *ajummas* grind up the mung beans by hand, using stone mills to create the paste for the pancake batter. The batter is then fried in batches on large sizzling griddles and the pancakes are piled high in front of their market stalls, to catch the eye of passing customers. The smell of these *bindaetteok* crisping up in the hot oil fills the market, making them impossible to resist.

We wanted to create our own take on these mung bean pancakes and decided to give them a South-Asian twist for a Korean/Indian pop-up that we held with some friends. The coconut adds a subtle sweetness, which provides a nice contrast to the tangy, sweet-and-spicy dipping sauce that we serve these with.

MAKES
8
PANCAKES

230g (8¼oz) yellow mung beans
350g (12oz) coconut milk
100g (3½oz) creamed coconut, grated
1 teaspoon salt

1½ teaspoons garam masala
1 onion, finely sliced
2 bird's eye chillies, finely sliced
vegetable oil, for frying

DIPPING SAUCE
2 bird's eye chillies, finely sliced
3 tablespoons apple vinegar
2 tablespoons caster sugar
½ tablespoon *gochugaru* (Korean red chilli powder)

1_ Put the mung beans in a bowl, cover with water and leave to soak for 4 hours.

2_ Meanwhile, for the dipping sauce, mix all the ingredients together in a bowl. Set aside.

3_ Once soaked, rinse and drain the mung beans, then tip them into a food processor with the coconut milk, creamed coconut, salt and garam masala and blend together to form a smooth batter. Stir the onion and chillies into the batter with a wooden spoon.

4_ Heat 2 tablespoons of vegetable oil in a large frying pan over a medium heat. Pour a ladleful (about 120ml/4fl oz) of batter into the pan and spread out to a 1-cm (½-inch) thickness. Fry for 2 minutes on each side until crispy and golden.

5_ Slide the pancake out of the pan and drain on kitchen paper while you continue to make the rest, adding an extra 2 tablespoons of oil to the pan for each pancake. Serve immediately with the dipping sauce.

Pa-Jeori SPRING ONION SALAD

My mum is from Busan, so I've always thought that this dish was called *Pa-Jeo-Leg-Gi*. That is, until I was teased about it recently. Korea has different accents and dialects, and this is just one example of the many words from Busan creeping into my Korean without me realising. The official name that you'll see on restaurant menus is *Pa-Jeori*. Whichever way you say it, these spicy spring onions make a great accompaniment to a Korean BBQ — the slightly vinegary dressing contrasting perfectly with the fatty meats and sweet marinades.

SERVES
4
AS A BANCHAN

200g (7oz) spring onions, trimmed
2 tablespoons regular soy sauce
2 garlic cloves, minced
2 tablespoons *gochugaru* (Korean red chilli powder)

2 teaspoons sesame oil
2 tablespoons caster sugar
2 tablespoons apple vinegar
1 teaspoon salt

1_ Cut the spring onions into 10-cm (4-inch) lengths, then cut each piece in half lengthways. Slice the spring onion halves lengthways as thin as you possibly can so that you have lots of fine spring onion strands.

2_ Place the spring onion strands in a large bowl with all the remaining ingredients. Using your fingertips, mix the ingredients together well for 2–3 minutes, until the spring onions are softened and completely coated and serve.

Gyeran Jjim FLUFFY STEAMED EGG

This dish is so simple but so delicious, and is one of my favourite *banchan*. The egg becomes really light and fluffy like a soufflé, lightly seasoned by the fermented shrimp. If the idea of seeing the whole little shrimp puts you off, either chop them up before you add them to the egg or use a good pinch of salt instead.

SERVES
4
AS A BANCHAN

3 eggs
approx. 200ml (7fl oz) water
1½ spring onions, trimmed and chopped

½ teaspoon vegetable oil
2 teaspoons *saeujeot* (salted fermented shrimp)

1_ Crack the eggs into a measuring jug, making a note of the volume of egg (this should be about 200ml/7fl oz but will vary depending on the eggs you use). Top up with the same quantity of water as egg, add half the spring onions and whisk together well.

2_ Brush the bottom of a heatproof earthenware dish or Korean *dolsot* stone bowl with the vegetable oil and place over a high heat.

3_ Add the egg mixture to the dish and cook for 3–4 minutes, whisking continuously, until the egg thickens to a custard-like consistency. Whisk the fermented shrimp into the mixture and cook for a further 1 minute, until the egg is just beginning to set and is starting to come away from the sides of the dish.

4_ Remove from the heat, spoon into a serving bowl and garnish with the remaining spring onions. Serve immediately.

A generic term for anything that has been mixed in seasoning, *muchim* are commonplace on a Korean dinner table as *banchan*. These dishes can always be found in our refrigerator at home – my mum will often grab a small handful of each and mix them together with rice and sesame oil to make a very quick *bibimbap* (mixed rice) but they can also be served as individual dishes.

In Korea, there's a phrase, '*son mat*', which means 'taste of the hand.' It refers to a person's natural ability to balance flavours to create a dish. The *muchim* recipes that feature here are my versions, but everyone makes them slightly differently, so feel free to tweak them to your own taste. Funnily enough, it's actually easiest to mix all the ingredients together by hand rather than a spoon, as it means you really rub the flavours into the vegetables and encourage their natural juices to form the marinade.

Sigeumchi Muchim SEASONED SPINACH

▮ Lightly seasoned, the sesame flavourings give the earthy spinach a subtle, nutty fragrance.

SERVES
6
AS A BANCHAN

400g (14oz) spinach leaves
½ teaspoon salt
1 small garlic clove, minced

1 teaspoon sesame oil
pinch of pepper
1 tablespoon roasted sesame seeds

1_ Bring a large saucepan of water to the boil.

2_ Add the spinach to the water and cook for 1 minute until wilted. Drain and rinse under cold running water, then squeeze out any excess water with your hands.

3_ Put the spinach in a bowl, add the remaining ingredients, and mix together with your hands, ensuring the spinach is thoroughly coated in the seasoning mixture. This will keep in the refrigerator for 3–4 days.

Kongnamul Muchim SEASONED BEAN SPROUTS

▮ An essential for *Dolsot Bibimbap* (see page 167), these beansprouts have a nice crunchy texture and are a staple banchan at most Korean tables.

SERVES
6
AS A BANCHAN

600g (1lb 5oz) bean sprouts
2 tablespoons salt
4 spring onions, trimmed and finely sliced

2 garlic cloves, minced
1 tablespoon roasted sesame seeds
1 tablespoon sesame oil

1_ Remove any brown heads and skins from the bean sprouts and cut off all the stringy roots.

2_ Fill a large saucepan with water and bring to the boil. Reduce the heat to a simmer, add the bean sprouts and cook for 5 minutes until tender. Drain and rinse under cold running water.

3_ Tip the bean sprouts into a large bowl and add all the remaining ingredients. Mix everything together with your hands, ensuring the bean sprouts are thoroughly coated in the seasoning mixture. This will keep in the refrigerator for 3–4 days.

Miyuk Muchim SEASONED SEAWEED

Probably my mum's favourite *muchim*, this seaweed *banchan* still retains the taste of the sea with a very savoury edge from the onions.

SERVES
6
AS A BANCHAN

25g (1oz) dried *miyuk* (wakame) seaweed
1 tablespoon vegetable oil
½ onion, finely sliced

pinch of salt
2 teaspoons sesame oil
2 tablespoons sesame seeds

1 teaspoon light soy sauce
1 small garlic clove, minced

1_ Put the seaweed in a small bowl, cover with cold water and leave for 10–15 minutes until soft and slippery. Drain, squeezing out any excess water with your hands, then roughly chop.

2_ Heat the oil in a heavy-based frying pan over a medium heat. Add the onion and salt and fry for 2–3 minutes, until the onion has softened but not coloured.

3_ Tip the onion into a large bowl and add the chopped seaweed, sesame oil, sesame seeds, soy sauce and garlic. Using your fingertips, mix the ingredients together well, ensuring the seaweed is thoroughly coated in the seasoning mixture. This will keep in the refrigerator for 3–4 days.

TIP: If you fancy something spicier, leave out the onions and soy sauce and mix in a couple of tablespoons of *Cho Gochujang* (see page 18) when combining the rest of the ingredients. This will make a spicy, sweet and sour sea weed *muchim* called *miyuk cho muchim*.

SIGEUMCHI MUCHIM

MIYUK MUCHIM

KONGNAMUL MUCHIM

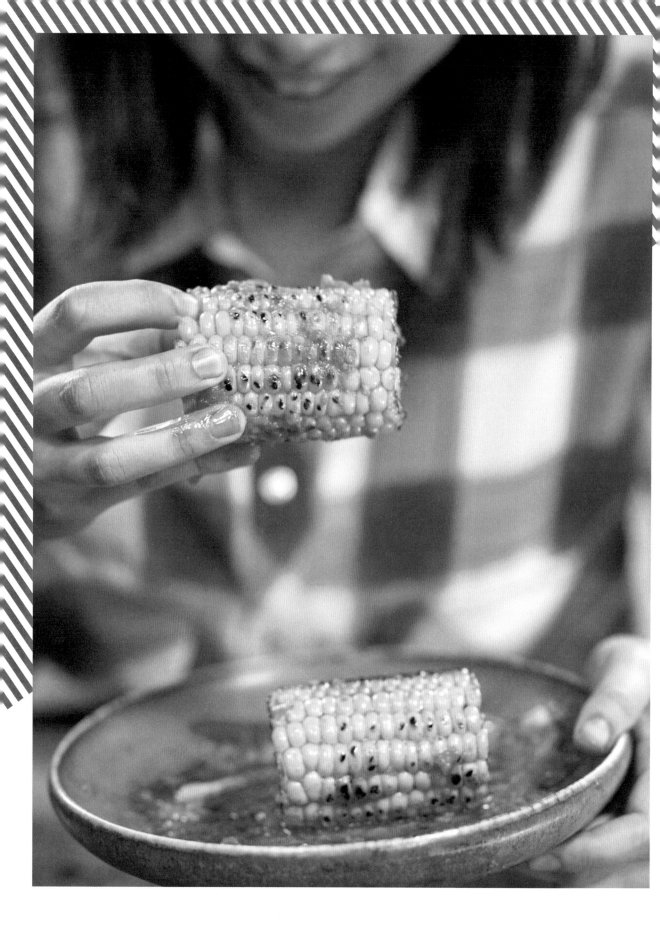

Corn on the Cob with Kimchi Butter

Oozing with melted butter, corn on the cob has to be one of the ultimate side dishes and the perfect accompaniment to a BBQ. Our *Kimchi* Butter, slathered on top, packs the corn full of salty, spicy flavours. Be generous with it, you'll want loads.

SERVES
8
AS A BANCHAN

4 sweetcorn, husks removed and halved
2 tablespoons vegetable oil
½ teaspoon salt

KIMCHI BUTTER
200g (7oz) *Baechu Kimchi* (see page 32), drained
250g (9oz) salted butter, softened

2 teaspoons fish sauce
4 garlic cloves, minced
1 tablespoon *gochujang* (Korean red chilli paste)

1_ To make the *kimchi* butter, put all the ingredients in a bowl. Mix everything together well with a wooden spoon (or use your hands if you prefer) until the ingredients are incorporated evenly through the butter.

2_ Tip the butter onto a chopping board covered in a sheet of clingfilm and form into a long sausage shape about 5cm (2 inches) in diameter. Wrap the clingfilm tightly around the butter, twisting the edges to seal, and refrigerate until needed.

3_ When you are ready to cook the sweetcorn, mix the vegetable oil together with the salt in a small bowl.

4_ Heat a cast-iron griddle pan over a medium heat. Brush the sweetcorn with the oil mixture, then add to the pan and cook for 10–12 minutes, turning with a pair of tongs and brushing with more oil every few minutes to ensure they cook evenly, until the kernels become swollen and start to make a popping noise.

5_ Flip the sweetcorn up on their ends and cook for 30 seconds on each end to sear and ensure all the corn kernels are cooked. Transfer to a large serving dish.

6_ Cut the *kimchi* butter into discs and slather all over the corn to serve.

TIP: Although you'll want to use loads of butter here, any left over will keep in the freezer for up to a month.

Ga-ji Bokkeum STIR-FRIED CHILLI AUBERGINE

I love the way aubergines act like sponges and soak up other flavours, and I particularly enjoy them when they're stir-fried. In this dish it's really important to salt and squeeze the aubergines first, so make sure not to skip this step – it will transform the aubergine from the sludgy stuff-of-nightmares to the beautifully caramelized, slightly sticky pieces you're after here.

SERVES
4
AS A BANCHAN

1 aubergine, trimmed
½ tablespoon salt
1 tablespoon vegetable oil

SAUCE
6 garlic cloves, minced
2 tablespoons *doenjang* (Korean soybean paste)
½ tablespoon clear runny honey
½ teaspoon sesame oil
½ tablespoon sesame seeds

pinch of pepper
1 tablespoon regular soy sauce
½ tablespoon mirin
1½ long chillies, trimmed and finely chopped
1 spring onion, trimmed and finely chopped

1_ For the sauce, put all the ingredients in a small bowl and mix together well. Set aside.

2_ Slice the aubergine in half lengthways, then slice each half into quarters so that you end up with eight long strips. Cut each strip into 7-cm (2¾-inch) long pieces.

3_ Put the aubergine pieces in a large bowl and cover with the salt. Leave for 15 minutes to draw out any excess water, then squeeze the pieces by hand to dry further (it's easiest to do this a few pieces at a time).

4_ Heat the vegetable oil in a frying pan over a high heat. Add the aubergines pieces and fry, stirring occasionally, for 4–5 minutes, until the flesh is softened and caramelized. Reduce the heat to medium, stir in the sauce to coat the aubergine pieces and fry for a further 3 minutes. This will keep in the refrigerator for 3 days.

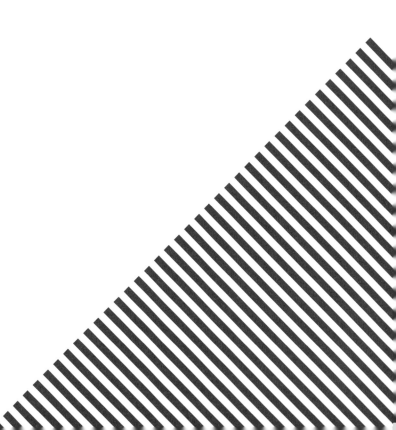

Gamja (Potato) Salad

Surprisingly, potato salad is one of those dishes that you often find at Korean restaurants, served alongside the *kimchi* as *banchan*. To be honest, it's never been one of my favourite choices as it's usually very heavy on mayonnaise and doesn't tend to have much flavour. This moreish version however, with its additions of smoky bacon, sharp mustard and tangy soured cream, will have everyone fighting over the last potato.

SERVES
4
AS A BANCHAN

1kg (2lb 4oz) new potatoes
1 tablespoon salt
3 smoked streaky bacon rashers, finely sliced

2 spring onions, trimmed and finely sliced
200ml (7fl oz) soured cream
½ teaspoon English mustard

pinch of pepper
1 small garlic clove, minced

1_ Cut any large potatoes in half so that they are all roughly the same size.

2_ Bring a large saucepan of water to the boil. Add the salt and potatoes, reduce the heat to a simmer and cook for 10–15 minutes, or until the potatoes are tender when pierced with a knife. Drain, rinse under cold running water to cool, then tip into a bowl. Set aside.

3_ Heat a frying pan over a medium heat. Add the bacon slices and cook, stirring, for 2–3 minutes, until lightly browned and crispy. Remove from the heat.

4_ Add the bacon to the potatoes, making sure to include all the crispy bits from the pan along with any rendered fat. Add the remaining ingredients and toss together well until the potatoes are completely coated in the dressing. Leave to cool and eat at room temperature.

Myulchi Bokkeum CANDIED ANCHOVIES

You know that saying, 'Mother knows best'? Well, in this case, my mum really does. I first tried making a version of this (actually very easy) side dish at home, and the result was slightly burnt, quite bitter and very salty. So, I called my mum for her recipe and here it is — her way produces sticky, crispy anchovies with a great chilli kick. Traditionally, these anchovies would be served in the middle of the table alongside some *kimchi* and lots of other *banchan*, but Gareth insists that they also make a great beer snack.

SERVES
6-8
AS A BANCHAN

1 tablespoon vegetable oil
50g (1¾oz) small dried anchovies,
    about 2-cm (¾-inch) long
2 bird's eye chillies, trimmed and finely sliced

3 tablespoons regular soy sauce
3 tablespoons corn syrup
1 tablespoon water

1_ Heat the vegetable oil in a heavy-based frying pan over a medium heat. Add the dried anchovies and chillies to the pan and fry for 1 minute, stirring to ensure the fish are evenly coated in the oil. Tip the anchovies and chillies out onto a plate and set aside.

2_ Return the frying pan to the heat and add the soy sauce, corn syrup and water. Simmer for 1–2 minutes, stirring to prevent the liquid catching on the bottom of the pan, until it has reduced to a thick, sticky syrup.

3_ Add the anchovies and chillies back to the pan and mix together with a wooden spoon to ensure they are evenly coated, then remove from the heat and spoon into a suitable container. Leave to cool, then cover and store in the refrigerator for up to a week until needed.

TIP: For a very quick, hassle-free dinner simply mix these anchovies through a little cooked rice.

Ya-che Ssam Moo PICKLED MOOLI PARCELS

I had these tangy little mooli parcels at my cousin's house in Seoul. It was the first time we'd visited her place since she'd got married and she served them as a starter – very unusual for Korean food! While they might not pack the big punchy flavours of some other Korean dishes (though the mustard dipping sauce gives them a lovely kick) they are beautifully crisp and fresh and make the perfect canapé if you're having a party, or a lovely light starter before a heavy meal.

SERVES
8
AS A BANCHAN

4 spring onions
20 pickled mooli slices (see Tip)
1 carrot, halved and cut into thin strips
1 red pepper, cut into thin strips

1 baby gem lettuce heart, finely chopped

DIPPING SAUCE
1 teaspoon caster sugar
1½ teaspoons English mustard or wasabi

1 tablespoon apple vinegar
1 teaspoon regular soy sauce

1_ Slice the green parts of the spring onions lengthways to create long thin strips. Discard the white parts.

2_ Mix all the dipping sauce ingredients together in a small bowl. Set aside.

3_ Arrange a few carrot and pepper strips in the centre of one mooli slice and top with a small pinch of chopped lettuce.

4_ Roll the mooli into a cigar-shaped parcel, tucking in the vegetables (don't worry if the some poke out the end). Tie a spring onion strip around the middle of your parcel to hold everything in place, then repeat with the rest of your mooli slices and filling ingredients.

5_ Arrange the mooli parcels on a large plate and serve with the dipping sauce.

TIP: Pickled mooli slices can be bought at most Korean stores and come in round packs, but if you can't get hold of these, you can make your own: shave a mooli with a vegetable peeler into long, wide ribbons, then cut these into 10-cm (4-inch) lengths and pickle using our Simple Pickle Brine recipe (see page 82). Don't feel bound by the choice of veg for the filling here either – use whatever crunchy veg you have to hand.

Mooli Slaw

We usually serve this as a topping for our *Jeyuk Bokkeum* (see page 108) pork belly buns. The pork belly is quite spicy, so the fresh and crunchy slaw gives it a cooling, refreshing contrast. If you leave this slaw to sit, the vegetables will release too much liquid, making it watery, so for best results be sure to eat it straight after making.

SERVES
4
AS A BANCHAN

350g (12oz) mooli, coarsely grated
1 carrot, grated
5 tablespoons apple vinegar

5 tablespoons natural yogurt
pinch of salt

1_ Put the grated mooli in a salad spinner and spin to get rid of any excess liquid. Drain and repeat until the mooli is quite dry.

2_ Put the mooli in a bowl, add the remaining ingredients and mix together thoroughly. Serve immediately.

YA-CHE SSAM MOO

Pickles & Sauces

ASK

THEN

GO

Even on a road

YOU

KNOW

No one likes dry food. Food should be moist, juicy and (in Gareth's opinion) covered in plenty of sauce. The Big Mac 'special sauce' is what gives the burger its tang and keeps it moist. Some people think so much of it that McDonald's was able to recently auction off a batch of 200 bottles of it for $20,000. While that seems a little crazy, I guess it goes to show how much some people appreciate a good sauce...

Just as the *jang* ingredients in the basics section represent the backbone of Korean cooking, the sauces here represent the backbone of our street food twist on Korean food.

Ssamjang Mayo

We top our burgers with *Ssamjang* Mayo (see page 83) to give them that salty earthiness that you typically get with *ssamjang* in a barbecue wrap. Mixing it with mayo makes it a little less intense, but it gives the burger an extra depth of flavour and makes a really great dipping sauce for fries.

Sweet Chilli Sauce

Our Korean Sweet Chilli Sauce (see page 86), or 'chicken sauce' as we usually call it on our trailer, is sweet, garlicky and a touch spicy. It's based on the best fried chicken sauces we've had in Korea and is just delicious slathered over everything.

Mehwah Jam

The *Mehwah* Jam (see page 85) or 'spicy jam' we make is full of fiery heat from the Scotch bonnet chilli, but is sticky and sweet too. This combination of sugar and intense heat makes it really addictive, and it goes so well with cheese. Gareth actually made a very similar jam for our wedding, where we had an evening buffet of cured meats, cheeses and pies – this spicy jam is the perfect accompaniment to anything like this.

Pickle Brine

We love *kimchi*, but it can sometimes be a little too punchy when eaten with certain dishes, which is when we like to use other pickles instead. Pickles are often eaten in Korea as they are a good way to preserve vegetables. Vegetables can be pickled in *gochujang*, in soy sauce or simply with sugar and vinegar, to create a nice, sharp contrast against any heavier foods. With fried chicken, for example, mooli that's very simply pickled is the perfect accompaniment as it is clean and fresh. We've found that the Pickle Brine (see page 82) that we use for mooli works really well with other veg too. We had to include it here as it gives vegetables a really nice refreshing zing but isn't so overpowering that you can't taste their natural flavours. It's the simplest recipe to remember and is a great one to have up your sleeve.

Mustard Pickled Onions

These pickled onions are a popular accompaniment to Korean BBQ, as the tangy vinegar cuts against the (often sweet) marinades and heavy meats. We top our burgers with them for the same reason, and they also make a great side for cold cuts, particularly the *Gochujang* Meatloaf (see page 110). While onions in Korea are very mild and are often eaten raw, regular brown onions can be a little more pungent, so we tend to soak them before pickling to get rid of any harsh flavours.

MAKES 1 SMALL JAR

2 onions, finely sliced
pinch of salt
100g (3½oz) English mustard

75g (2½oz) caster sugar
125ml (4fl oz) apple vinegar

1_ Put the onions in a bowl and cover with water. Add the salt and leave to soak for 10 minutes.

2_ Meanwhile, in a separate large bowl, mix together the mustard, sugar and apple vinegar.

3_ Once soaked, drain the onions and add them to the mustard sauce. Mix together thoroughly so that the onions are completely coated. Either eat immediately or, for best results, transfer to a small jar and leave in the refrigerator for 24 hours to soften.

Zingy Green Sauce

This zingy sauce is not very Korean at all – in fact, both limes and coriander are difficult to get hold of in Korea – yet it works fantastically well with Korean BBQ. One winter, we collaborated with our friends Ben and Aneesha to hold an Indian/Korean night at a local restaurant. As we tested lots of different recipe ideas, we were surprised to discover all the overlaps between the two cuisines (think chutneys, pickles and spices), and their Indian green chutney was one of my highlights of the night. This recipe adds a delicious freshness to any dish and makes a perfect partner for our *Kimchi* Salsa (see below) as a dipping sauce.

MAKES APPROX
375g
(13OZ)

200g (7oz) coriander leaves and stalks
2 spring onions, trimmed
1 whole garlic clove

20g (½oz) fresh root ginger, peeled
½ long chilli (optional)
juice of 3½ limes, plus extra if needed

Put the coriander, spring onions, garlic, ginger and chilli, if using, in a food processor. Pour over the lime juice and blend until smooth, adding a little more lime juice if the sauce is looking too thick. Serve or keep refrigerated for up to 3 days.

Kimchi Salsa

Korean-Mexican food is really big in both Korea and America. The punchy flavours of both countries really complement each other, while Mexican salsas and sauces lend Korean foods a bright, zesty freshness. This tomato salsa has a subtle Korean tangy kick from the *kimchi*. It's quick and easy to prepare and makes a perfect accompaniment for Korean BBQ, as well as a great dipping sauce for Lotus Root Nachos (see page 215).

MAKES APPROX
375g
(13OZ)

2 tomatoes
½ red onion
2 tablespoons matured *Baechu Kimchi* (see page 32)

pinch of salt
2 tablespoons *gochugaru* (Korean red chilli powder)
small handful of coriander leaves, roughly chopped

Finely chop the tomatoes, red onion and *kimchi*. Transfer to a serving bowl, add the salt, *gochugaru* and coriander leaves and mix together well. Serve immediately.

Gochujang Ketchup

We had a huge batch of tomatoes in our refrigerator one day, so we decided to use them up by making a ketchup. Roasting the tomatoes and charring them a little gives them a nice smoky flavour that works really well with the *gochujang*. It's ketchup — you know what to do.

MAKES APPROX 650g (1LB 7OZ)

1kg (2lb 4oz) tomatoes, halved
1 onion, roughly chopped
1 teaspoon salt
3 tablespoons vegetable oil

1 long red chilli, trimmed and roughly chopped
6 garlic cloves, minced
3 tablespoons *gochujang* (Korean red chilli paste)
100ml (3½fl oz) apple vinegar

2 tablespoons regular soy sauce
65g (2½oz) soft brown sugar
2 tablespoons *gochugaru* (Korean red chilli powder)
50ml (2fl oz) water

1_ Preheat the oven to 180°C (350°F), Gas Mark 4.

2_ Put the tomato halves in a large bowl, add the onion, salt and 2 tablespoons of the vegetable oil and mix together well.

3_ Tip the tomato mixture onto a roasting tray, laying the tomato halves out flat to prevent them overlapping, and roast in the oven for 40 minutes until the tomatoes are softened and beginning to colour at the edges. Remove from the oven and leave to cool, then transfer to a food processor, add the chilli and blend together until silky smooth.

4_ Heat the remaining 1 tablespoon of vegetable oil in a heavy-based saucepan over a low heat. Add the garlic and fry for 1 minute until softened, then add the blended tomatoes along with all the remaining ingredients. Bring to a simmer, cover and leave to cook for 20 minutes.

5_ Strain the ketchup through a sieve, discarding the pulp, and pour into a large clean jar. Store in the refrigerator for up to a week.

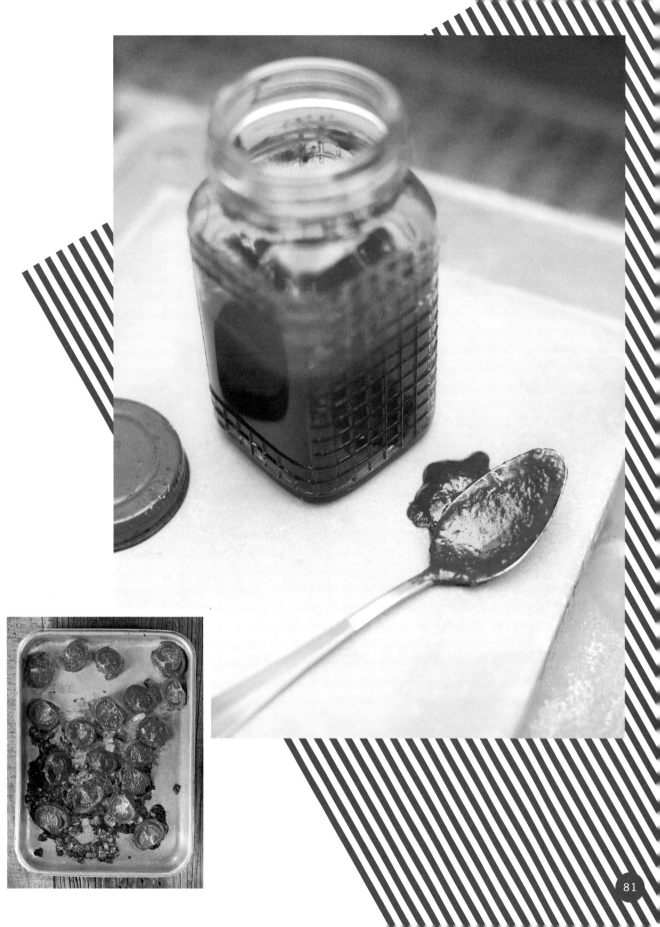

Simple Pickle Brine

This simple pickle brine is traditionally used to make the pickled *moo* (Korean radish) cubes that are served at almost every fried chicken shop in Korea. We use it a lot on our trailer and for events, as it's subtle, clean and refreshing – our favourites include apple and chilli pickle, pickled mooli cubes and pickled cauliflower – though it works with pretty much any vegetable.

The recipe works as follows:

1_ Mix together equal parts caster sugar, water and apple vinegar, making enough to cover whatever vegetable you plan on pickling.

2_ Put your chosen veg in a suitable container, cover with the brine, then leave in the refrigerator for at least 24 hours.

It's that simple!

Really Great Cheese Sauce

There are so many uses for this cheese sauce – you can top your burgers with it, stir it into cooked pasta, or eat it as a cheese fondue, the choice is yours. The amount of chilli powder and garlic used here might be tiny but they make all the difference, their subtle background flavour transforming the sauce from being just something rich and heavy into something really moreish.

MAKES APPROX
550g
(1 PINT)

50g (1¾oz) butter
50g (1¾oz) plain flour
400ml (14fl oz) whole milk, plus extra if needed
100g (3½oz) medium Cheddar cheese, grated

100g (3½oz) red Leicester cheese, grated
pinch of extra hot chilli powder
pinch of salt
1 garlic clove, minced

1_ Slowly melt the butter in a saucepan over a medium heat (don't rush this as you don't want the butter to colour). Add the flour to the butter and whisk together to form a smooth paste (roux). Continue to cook, stirring, for 2–3 minutes, then gradually add the milk, stirring constantly with a whisk to stop it from catching and becoming lumpy.

2_ Stir in the grated cheeses, then add the remaining ingredients, stirring, and cook for a further 2–3 minutes, until all the cheese is melted. If you feel the sauce is getting too thick, add another splash of milk to thin it out. This can be made in advance; heat through over a moderate heat (adding extra milk if necessary) when ready to use.

Ssamjang Mayo

Adding a touch of *ssamjang* to mayonnaise gives it a rounded umami depth that brings out all the meaty flavours of a burger. This slightly salty mayo is also a great dipping sauce for fries, especially when mixed together with *Mehwah* Jam (see page 85).

MAKES APPROX
200g
(7OZ)

200g (7oz) mayonnaise, either shop-bought or homemade (see below)

2 teaspoons *Ssamjang* (see page 21)
½ teaspoon sesame oil

Spoon the mayo into a bowl, add the *ssamjang* and sesame oil and stir to combine. Serve or keep refrigerated for up to 3 days.

Joe's Sauce

Our friend Joe runs Korea's biggest English-speaking food blog and is a fountain of Korean food knowledge, so when he told me about his award-winning paprika-spiked *gochujang* aioli sauce we had to give it a go. No surprise, it's delicious — perfect for whenever you'd usually eat aioli or plain mayo, and so much better than either. I never took down exact quantities though, so Joe, we hope you approve!

MAKES APPROX
240g
(9OZ)

200g (7oz) mayonnaise, either shop-bought or homemade (see method)
1 tablespoon smoked paprika
6 garlic cloves, minced
2 tablespoons *gochujang* (Korean red chilli paste)

2 tablespoons lemon juice

HOMEMADE MAYO
4 egg yolks
½ teaspoon English mustard

pinch of salt
1 tablespoon apple vinegar
200ml (7fl oz) vegetable oil

1_ To make the mayo, put the egg yolks, mustard, salt and apple vinegar in a food processor and blend together. With the motor running, pour in the vegetable oil in a thin, stready stream until you have a thick, creamy mayonnaise.

2_ Spoon the mayo into a bowl, add the remaining ingredients and stir together well. Serve or keep refrigerated for up to 3 days.

Mehwah Jam FIERY SCOTCH BONNET CHILLI JAM

As our burgers are quite mildly flavoured, we wanted to offer something that could help them pack a bit of extra punch. Enter our *Mehwah* Jam – made with Scotch bonnets so it's definitely fiery, but also sweet and sticky too. While I like to add it to our burgers (I simply can't resist a chilli burger), to be honest, I eat it with pretty much anything. In fact, my favourite way to eat it is spread over cool, creamy goats' cheese on top of crispy crackers. Make a batch of this jam and you'll soon be scouring your cupboards looking for things to eat it with too.

MAKES APPROX 450g (1LB)

320g (11½oz) Scotch bonnet chillies
100g (3½oz) caster sugar
100g (3½oz) soft brown sugar

250ml (9fl oz) apple vinegar
pinch of salt

1_ Wearing disposable gloves, cut the tops off the chillies and discard. Put the chillies in a food processor and blend together for 30–40 seconds to form a rough paste.

2_ Tip the chilli paste into a saucepan, add the remaining ingredients and bring to a boil. Boil for 15 minutes uncovered (it's a good idea to have your extractor fan on as these chillies are pretty potent), stirring occasionally, until the liquid has reduced by two-thirds and is thick and jammy in consistency.

3_ Pour into a sterilized jar and leave to cool. Store in the refrigerator for up to a month.

Korean Sweet Chilli Sauce

This is our take on a Korean sweet chilli sauce, so you can use it as a table sauce to dip your fries into, or just eat it with pretty much... anything. We call this 'chicken sauce' on our trailer, as we pour it all over our Korean Fried Chicken (see page 212) and *Ramyun* Chicken Buns (see page 118).

MAKES ABOUT
1l
(1¾ PINTS)

3 tablespoons vegetable oil
12 garlic cloves, minced
60g (2¼oz) tomato ketchup
60g (2¼oz) *gochujang* (Korean red chilli paste)

125ml (4fl oz) corn syrup
3 tablespoons *gochugaru* (Korean red chilli powder)
3 tablespoons apple vinegar

1_ Heat the oil in a large frying pan over a medium-high heat. Add the garlic and fry for 2–3 minutes, until softened. Add the rest of the ingredients and cook for another 5–6 minutes, until the sauce starts bubbling at the edges. Remove from the heat.

2_ Leave to cool, then pour into clean, sterilized bottles. Store in the refrigerator for up to a month.

Maneul Jangajji SOY-PICKLED GARLIC

Pickling vegetables in soy sauce is a popular way to preserve them in Korea. Through pickling in soy sauce, garlic cloves lose their harsh flavours and instead become quite sweet and tangy. I love eating this thinly sliced on top of slow-cooked braises such as *Sogogi Gori Jjim* (see page 143), the sweetness of the pickled garlic lifting the flavour of the rich meat.

MAKES
1
SMALL JAR

50 whole garlic cloves

FIRST BRINE
500ml (18fl oz) apple vinegar
250ml (9fl oz) water
120g (4oz) salt

SOY BRINE
125ml (4fl oz) regular soy sauce
250ml (9fl oz) Step 1 Brine
150g (5½oz) caster sugar
250ml (9fl oz) water

1_ Combine the First Brine ingredients in a sealable container. Add the garlic, cover and leave in the refrigerator for 5 days (don't worry if your garlic turns blue at this stage, it is simply reacting with the vinegar and is still safe to eat).

2_ After 5 days, drain the garlic, reserving 250ml (9fl oz) of the brining liquid. Set the garlic aside.

3_ Pour the reserved brining liquid into a small saucepan over a medium heat. Add the soy brine ingredients and simmer for 10 minutes, then pour back into the sealable container. Add the garlic, seal and refrigerate for 10 days before eating.

Korean Meat & BBQ

05

Even the MOON Wanes WHEN IT'S FULL

As we mentioned earlier, Korean BBQ is rarely eaten at home, but it's still a very important part of Korean culture. There are Korean BBQ restaurants lining almost every street in Seoul, and competition is fierce.

Korean BBQ is very much about a shared dining experience and most people will go to eat Korean BBQ in large groups (whether that be with family, friends or with work colleagues), while a lot of restaurants will turn you away if you want Korean BBQ for one. Meat is chosen collectively by the group as it's shared by the whole table, with most restaurants in Korea specializing in a particular meat or even cut. The meat is either offered plain, seasoned with a little salt or marinated in either a soy-based sauce (such as *Bulgogi* Sauce, see page 95) or *gochujang*. The meat is then served to the table on a large platter, and then it's down to the youngest in the group (within reason) to be in charge of the grill and make sure that the meat is properly cooked for the rest of the table. This is as a sign of respect, as the person cooking usually has the least chance of getting to eat much meat.

The grill is set in the middle of the table (often with space-age style extractor tubes coming down from the ceiling to get rid of the smoke) and everyone helps themselves once it's cooked, making their own lettuce wraps and filling them with the meat and their other chosen fillings. Nowadays, some 'fusion' BBQ restaurants have adopted special grills for the centre of the barbecue with reservoirs around the edges, for cooking eggs or cheese in the meaty juices. I have to admit, I'm still not used to these quite yet – cheese feels like an unusual addition and I prefer the more authentic restaurants. A lot of our favourite types of Korean BBQ are the simple, unmarinated meats.

Korea has many more cuts of meat compared to the UK, so you might have to ask your butcher to see if they can help you if you're after a particular Korean cut. Koreans tend to like meats that have a lot of marbling to them for maximum flavour – and often tend to prefer chewier cuts to the ones we're used to (Gareth calls this 'the Korean chew'). Korean people have a saying called *shibnen mat* (literally 'chewing flavour') which refers to the flavour you get from chewing your food – as they often like to feel that they're properly chewing on something when they're eating. Pork and beef are the most popular meats when it comes to Korean BBQ – other meats such as chicken, duck and sometimes shellfish are also eaten on occasion, but much more rarely.

BEEF

Beef is quite expensive in Korea, much more so than pork. It's probably for this reason that Korea has so many different cuts of beef – around 120 in total – so that the whole cow can really be appreciated and enjoyed. Some of the most popular cuts include:

Deungshim (Rib Eye)

This juicy cut is a popular choice for barbecue as it's tender, juicy and has good marbling. The *deungshim* is sliced very thinly so that it cooks quickly.

Anshim (Tenderloin)

Anshim is an expensive cut of meat, cut from the loin of the cow. This part doesn't do a lot of work so it's very tender and mild in flavour.

Chadolbaegi (Brisket)

Chadolbaegi are wafer-thin slices of beef brisket. They are full of marbling, so tend to cause the flames to spark up from underneath as soon as they hit the grill.

Galbi Sal (Rib Meat)

Galbi sal are thin strips of rib meat and are one of the most popular cuts for Korean BBQ as they're less expensive than the other beef cuts, but still have good flavour.

Galbi (Short Ribs)

Korean beef ribs are cut differently to the ones you'd normally get in the UK. They take the middle short ribs and cut through the bone, and then open up the meat, without detaching it, so that there's one long strip of beef attached to a chunk of bone at the end. Often when barbecuing, this chunk of bone is cut using a pair of scissors so that all the meat cooks evenly, and the rib can be enjoyed later as it has a longer cooking time.

LA *Galbi* (Laterally-cut Beef Ribs)

With LA *galbi* the beef is cut lengthways through the rib bones to create a long, thin strip of beef with a line of rib bones along the top.

PORK

Pork is the most popular meat in Korea by a long way as it's much cheaper than beef, and most people prefer the fattier cuts because of their flavour and texture.

Samgyeopsal (Pork Belly)

Samgyeopsal translates as 'three-layered meat' (*sam* means three in Korean), due to the layers of fat. Very thinly sliced, this is the most popular Korean cut, though some people can find it a little too rich.

Ogyeopsal (Pork Belly)

Ogyeopsal translates as 'five-layered meat,' (*o* means five in Korean). It's cut from the pork belly, just like *samgyeopsal*, but this part also includes an extra meaty layer with extra pig skin.

Hangjeongsal (Front Neck)

We tried *hanjeongsal* for the first time on our most recent trip to Korea and wish that we'd had it sooner. *Hanjeongsal* is cut from the front part of the neck, has lots of marbling and is incredibly tender and juicy.

Galmegisal (Skirt Meat)

Galmegisal is taken from right under the ribs. In the UK, this part would usually be ground up as sausage meat, discarded, or frozen and sent to Asia, which is such a waste as it's our favourite cut of meat. It could easily be mistaken for beef as it's a dark meat that's rich in flavour and quite lean. *Galmegisal* should be grilled whole over a charcoal barbecue until just cooked through and still a little pink. At this point it should be cut into bite-sized pieces to finish cooking. Gareth's favourite barbecue place in Seoul suggests dipping each piece into a lemon mustard dipping sauce followed by a little bit of roasted soybean powder, then wrapping it in a lettuce leaf with some *ssamjang* and a smoky barbecued mushroom. If you can get hold of some *galmegisal*, you have to try this – it's so good!

KOREAN BBQ AT HOME

On the occasions that we have Korean BBQ at home, we use a small camping stove that we place in the middle of the table. We then set our table as we would for most other Korean meals, with at least five or six different *banchan* (which would of course include *kimchi*), along with a soup or stew (in our house it would be *Doenjang Jjigae*, see page 141) and an individual bowl of rice for each person. We then lay out a big plate of assorted leaves (lollo rosso, Korean sesame leaves, baby gems and round lettuce are popular choices) and put some *Ssamjang* (see page 21) in the middle of the table, along with some hot chillies and raw garlic cloves. Koreans often eat garlic cloves raw as part of Korean BBQ, but you can also fashion a little cup out of aluminium foil, fill it with oil and then gently cook the garlic at the same time as the meat, without risking it burning.

For the barbecue itself, as well as the meat (and garlic), we would often add some other ingredients such as *kimchi* or mushrooms (usually enoki or king oyster), which take on a really nice, smoky flavour.

When it comes to wrapping and eating, the great thing about the Korean BBQ wrap (called *ssam*) is that you can really add whatever you like to your leaves. Most people though, would eat it like this:

- Take a lettuce leaf in the palm of your hand (I often like to layer a couple of different types of leaves)
- Add a small spoonful of rice (optional)
- If you're eating unmarinated meat, dip it in a little sesame oil and salt
- If you're eating marinated meat, put this straight on top of the lettuce leaf or rice
- Add a smear of *ssamjang*
- Add a slice of chilli or raw garlic on top (optional)
- Add a small pinch of *Pa-Jeori* (see page 57) or Mustard Pickled Onions (see page 76)
- Wrap the lettuce leaf tightly into as small a parcel as you can make it and pop the whole thing in your mouth.

As you have to stuff it in your mouth, Korean BBQ certainly doesn't make for the most attractive date food, but it's the best way to taste all the flavours at the same time. There's more to Korean food than just barbecue though, so we've included some other examples in this section. Some are meat dishes that have been inspired by the traditional barbecue marinades, such as our *Bulgogi* Burger (see page 96) whereas others are just our favourite Korean meat or fish dishes, most of which are designed to share in the middle of the table.

Kimchi Brine

This brine can lift a meat dish from good to amazing. It's based on the ingredients we use for *kimchi*, and is packed full of flavour but it also locks in all of the meat's moisture, so the end result is super-juicy. It's really easy to mix together, and is definitely worth making.

MAKES
1l
(1¾ PINTS)

3 long red chillies, trimmed and halved lengthways

12 garlic cloves, minced

5-cm (2-inch) piece of fresh root ginger, peeled and very finely chopped

1½ tablespoons salt

125ml (4fl oz) fish sauce

1 litre (1¾ pints) water

Mix all the ingredients together in a large bowl.

Bulgogi Sauce

Bulgogi sauce is traditionally used to marinate beef for Korean BBQ, as it really brings out the deep, meaty flavours. Traditional *bulgogi* sauce recipes usually include Asian pears (or sometimes other fruits), which sweeten the sauce and help to tenderize the meat. We use apple juice here to create the same fruity flavours but make a nice clear sauce, which we use for our burgers and Philly cheesesteaks.

MAKES ENOUGH FOR
1kg
(2LB 4OZ) OF BEEF

175ml (6fl oz) regular soy sauce
100g (3½oz) golden caster sugar
6 garlic cloves, minced

2-cm (¾-inch) piece of fresh root ginger, peeled and very finely chopped
1 tablespoon sesame oil

3 spring onions, trimmed and thinly sliced
200ml (7fl oz) clear apple juice

Mix all the ingredients together in a large bowl.

> **TIP:** If you're using this marinade for traditional Korean BBQ, use thin slices of featherblade or sirloin. Marinate the beef for at least 30 minutes before cooking and then grill over a high heat for 3–4 minutes, or until cooked to your liking.

Bulgogi Burger

Our *bulgogi* burger is one of the bestsellers on our menu and is where it all started for us on our truck. When we first started testing this burger, we quickly found that the traditional *bulgogi* sauce was too thin to stick to the burger patty, making it difficult to taste the flavour of the sauce. After a lot of experimenting, we found that adding a tiny bit of xanthan gum did the trick. A natural binding agent, xanthan gum doesn't have any flavour, it just acts to thicken the sauce – if you can't find any, use a little cornflour mixed with water instead.

MAKES
4
BURGERS

600g (1lb 5oz) minced beef (ideally coarse-ground, with 20 per cent fat)
pinch of salt
1 tablespoon vegetable oil

480ml (17fl oz) *Bulgogi* Sauce (see page 95)
½ tablespoon xanthan gum
4 bread buns

TO ASSEMBLE
4 tablespoons shredded iceberg lettuce
4 tablespoons Mustard Pickled Onions (see page 76)
120ml (4fl oz) *Ssamjang* Mayo (see page 83)

1_ Divide the minced beef into 4 even-sized portions. Being careful not to overwork the mince (otherwise the burgers will become dry), shape the portions into circular patties around 1.5 cm (⅝ inch) thick. Season both sides of each patty with the salt.

2_ Heat the vegetable oil in a large heavy-based frying pan over a medium heat. Add the burger patties and cook for 2–3 minutes on one side without moving or flipping them (you want to try and build a good crust on it for great flavour and texture). Flip the burger over and cook for a further 2 minutes on the other side, again without moving it around the pan.

3_ Put the *bulgogi* sauce and the xanthan gum into a small saucepan and whisk the xantham gum vigorously into the sauce. Continue whisking for 3–4 minutes until the sauce thickens then set to one side.

4_ Put the saucepan over a medium heat and keep stirring until the sauce thickens. Be careful not to boil otherwise the xanthan gum becomes gloopy.

5_ Slice the buns in half and lay them cut-side down in a large dry frying pan over a high heat, for 30–40 seconds, until warmed through and slightly charred at the edges.

6_ To assemble your burgers, arrange the shredded lettuce on the bottom bun halves. Dip the cooked patties into the warmed *bulgogi* sauce, then place them carefully on top of the lettuce. Pour over an extra tablespoon of the sauce (to make things really juicy), and spoon over the pickled onions. Smear the mayo over the inside of the top bun halves and pile on top of the burgers to finish.

Enjoy with plenty of napkins!

4

Bulgogi Philly Cheesesteak

We cooked these cheesesteaks at our very first pop-up on a cold night back in February 2014. At the time we thought they were great, but looking back we had never cooked so many dishes in such a short space of time, so we probably didn't do them justice. Since then, we've been working hard to perfect the recipe and we think this is it – the *bulgogi* sauce helps to bring out the beefy taste of the meat and the cheese sauce is finger-licking great. It's really important to use a chewy bread made from potato or rice flour here, as the sandwich has so much sauce that anything soft like a brioche bun will just fall apart (and be too sweet), while a baguette has too much crust. Great bread makes a great sandwich and you'll want something to soak up all that meaty juice.

SERVES
4

2½ tablespoons vegetable oil
generous knob of butter
1 onion, finely sliced
1 red pepper, cored, deseeded and finely sliced
150ml (¼ pint) *Bulgogi* Sauce (see page 95)

4 x 100g (3½oz) sirloin steaks, each about 1cm (½ inch) thick
4 potato or rice flour rolls, each about 10cm (4 inches) long, halved lengthways
250ml (9fl oz) Really Great Cheese Sauce (see page 82)

salt

TO GARNISH
2 spring onions, trimmed and thinly sliced
1 tablespoon *gochugaru* (Korean red chilli powder)

1_ Heat the oil and butter in a large frying pan over a medium heat. Add the onion, season with a pinch of salt and fry for 10 minutes, until the onion is silky soft and caramelized (be patient – great onions take time). Add the pepper and cook for 3 minutes until slightly softened, then remove the mix from the pan and set aside.

2_ Gently heat the *bulgogi* sauce in a small saucepan over a medium heat, being careful not to let it boil as it can make the sauce taste bitter. Meanwhile, heat the cheese sauce in a separate small saucepan over a medium heat, adding a little extra milk if it needs thinning. Set both aside.

3_ Place the frying pan over a very high heat until smoking. Add the steaks and cook for about 40 seconds on each side until cooked to your liking (you may need to do this in batches). Remove from the pan and leave to rest for 1 minute.

4_ While the steaks are resting, warm the bread roll halves by putting them cut-side down in the pan and heating them through for 30 seconds. Transfer the rolls to plates and spread the onion and pepper mixture over each half.

5_ Cut the steaks into 5-mm (¼-in) thick strips, add them to the saucepan with the *bulgogi* sauce and stir to coat evenly. Place the beef strips into the roll then spoon over the cheese sauce. Serve scattered with the spring onion slices and sprinkled with the *gochugaru* to garnish.

Yukhoe KOREAN STEAK TARTARE

Though we might be a little biased, this is definitely our favourite way of eating raw beef. Basically a Korean steak tartare, *yukhoe* is made from raw fillet steak that has been lightly marinated to become soft and tender. Flavoured with soy and sesame, this dish is very delicate, with the egg yolk acting as a sauce that binds everything together and the lovely balance of sweet and salty really bringing out the beef's natural flavours.

SERVES
2
AS A SHARING
DISH

1 x 200g (7oz) fillet steak
¼ Asian pear, peeled, cored and cut into fine
   matchsticks
1 egg yolk
½ teaspoon sesame seeds

½ teaspoon spring onion, trimmed and finely sliced

MARINADE
1 tablespoon regular soy sauce
½ tablespoon sesame oil
1 tablespoon roasted sesame seeds

½ tablespoon clear, runny honey
1 garlic clove, minced
½ spring onion, trimmed and finely sliced
pinch of salt

1_ For the marinade, mix together all the ingredients in a bowl. Set aside.

2_ Trim the beef fillet of any fat or sinew and cut it into wafer-thin slices using a sharp knife.

3_ Add the beef slices to the marinade bowl and mix them around with your fingertips to make sure they are completely coated. Add the pear and mix together.

4_ Place a large cookie cutter or chef's ring onto the centre of a plate. Spoon the beef mixture into the cutter or ring, pressing down on the edges. Carefully place the egg yolk in the middle.

5_ Remove the cutter or ring and serve scattered with the sesame seeds and spring onion.

LA Galbi KOREAN-STYLE SHORT RIBS

There's a bit of contention as to where the 'LA' in 'LA *Galbi*' comes from. Some say that it's proof that the dish originated among the Korean-American population of Los Angeles, others say it comes from the word 'lateral', because of the way the ribs are cut. Whichever is true, this dish is a popular choice for Korean BBQ and it's one we ate a lot as I was growing up.

SERVES
4

1.5kg (3lb 5oz) beef ribs, cut into LA *galbi*-style strips
  (see Tip)
1 tablespoon vegetable oil

MARINADE
2 spring onions, trimmed and finely chopped

½ Asian pear, peeled, cored and finely chopped
½ onion, finely chopped
12 garlic cloves, minced
5-cm (2-inch) piece of fresh root ginger, peeled and very
  finely chopped

pinch of pepper
200ml (7fl oz) regular soy sauce
2 tablespoons sesame oil
3 tablespoons soft brown sugar

1_ For the marinade, mix together all the ingredients in a bowl.

2_ Place the beef rib strips in a large dish. Pour over the marinade and mix together to ensure the ribs are evenly coated. Cover with clingfilm, transfer to the refrigerator and leave to marinate for at least 4 hours, preferably overnight.

3_ When you are ready to cook, heat a cast-iron griddle pan over a medium-high heat and brush it with the vegetable oil.

4_ Using a pair of tongs, lift the strips of beef out of the marinade, shaking off any excess. Lay the strips flat on the griddle and cook for 2–3 minutes on each side until slightly charred (you may need to do this in batches).

5_ Remove the rib strips from the pan and leave to cool slightly. Cut the strips at every second bone into smaller pieces to make them easier to pick up and eat.

TIP: For LA *galbi*-style ribs, ask your butcher to cut them thinly across the bone. This will give you long strips of beef with small discs of bone at the top – you can use these bones later as little handles to pick the *galbi* up and eat them by hand.

Donkasu CRISPY PORK ESCALOPE

There are many overlaps between Korean and Japanese cooking, and *donkasu* is just one example. Coming from the Japanese word *tonkatsu*, this hot, crispy, breaded pork escalope is served with a sticky brown sauce that tastes and looks a bit like a thicker version of Worcestershire sauce. The first time I tried it was during a summer in Jeju when I lived with my cousin Jisoo. She was about 12 at the time, and I remember her making me this dish for breakfast one morning. Admittedly, I was a little worried that she'd burn herself on the hot oil, or that the pork wouldn't be cooked through (it was the first time I'd ever seen her cook anything) but the *donkasu* she made was perfectly crispy and delicious and I remember her smiling with pride as she served it up. I've never seen Jisoo cook anything since, so she's either secretly a great cook, or this dish really is just that easy!

SERVES 2

2 x 150g (5½oz) pork escalopes
1 egg, beaten
5 tablespoons plain flour
5 tablespoons panko breadcrumbs
pinch of salt
pinch of ground white pepper

200ml (7fl oz) vegetable oil

SAUCE
3 tablespoons tomato ketchup
2 tablespoons caster sugar
1 tablespoon apple vinegar
2 tablespoons regular soy sauce

2 garlic cloves, minced
½ apple, puréed

TO SERVE
¼ white cabbage, shredded
160g (5¾oz) cooked short-grain rice (see page 26)

1_ For the sauce, put all the ingredients in a saucepan over a medium heat, bring to a simmer and cook, stirring occasionally, for 5–6 minutes until the sauce has thickened and easily coats the back of a wooden spoon. Remove from the heat and set aside.

2_ Using a rolling pin, pound the pork escalopes until they are about 1cm (½ inch) thick.

3_ Pour the beaten egg onto a large plate. Put the flour on a separate plate, smoothing it flat, then do the same with the breadcrumbs on a third plate.

4_ Season the pork escalopes on both sides with the salt and pepper. Take an escalope and dip it in the flour, then turn over to coat both sides. Shake off any excess flour, then repeat the process with the beaten egg and, lastly, the breadcrumbs, pressing the crumbs into the escalope with your fingertips to ensure they stick to the meat. Repeat with the second escalope.

5_ Heat the oil in a large frying pan over a medium heat to the point where a few breadcrumbs dropped into the pan will cause the oil to start to bubble. Gently lay the pork escalopes into the frying pan (to avoid overcrowding the pan you may need to do this in batches) and fry for 6–8 minutes, turning carefully halfway through cooking, until golden brown all over. Carefully remove the escalopes from the pan, transfer to a plate lined with kitchen paper to soak up any excess oil and leave to cool for 2 minutes.

6_ To serve, gently heat the sauce and spoon the rice into bowls. Cut the escalopes diagonally into 1-cm (½-inch) pieces, pushing the knife directly down on top of the pork escalope rather than sliding it back and forth to avoid knocking off any of the crispy breadcrumbs, and lay over the cooked rice. Pour over the sauce and accompany with the shredded cabbage.

TIP: Panko breadcrumbs can be found in most Asian supermarkets or easily online. If you can't get hold of them, you can use regular dried breadcrumbs instead, though you won't get quite the same crunch.

Sticky, Spicy Pork Ribs

These ribs are a tender, juicy, joy to eat. In fact, they're so good, we've even managed to convince our friends to help us move house on the promise of payment with them a couple of times. If you want to use these ribs as a new form of currency like this, just boil them up and pop them in a ziplock bag full of the sauce the night before, then finish them in your new oven as you kick back and enjoy a well-deserved beer the following day.

SERVES
2

500g (1lb 2oz) pork spare ribs
50g (1¾oz) fresh root ginger, roughly chopped
5 whole garlic cloves, peeled
125ml (4fl oz) light soy sauce
2 spring onions, trimmed and finely chopped, to garnish

SAUCE
1 tablespoon sesame oil
4 tablespoons *gochujang* (Korean red chilli paste)
4 tablespoons apricot jam
1 tablespoon regular soy sauce
1 tablespoon honey

1 tablespoon roasted sesame seeds
1 tablespoon white rice vinegar
8 garlic cloves, minced
5-cm (2-inch) piece of fresh root ginger, peeled and very finely chopped

---

1_ Put the ribs in a large saucepan or stockpot with the ginger, garlic, soy sauce and enough water to cover. Bring to the boil, reduce the heat to a simmer and leave to cook gently for 1½ hours, until the ribs are tender and cooked through.

2_ Meanwhile, combine all the sauce ingredients in a bowl and mix together well. Line an oven tray with foil (this will make everything a lot easier to wash up later) and preheat the oven to 200°C (400°F), Gas Mark 6.

3_ Arrange the cooked ribs on the prepared tray and brush with the sauce to coat evenly. Roast in the oven for 20 minutes, turning and basting the ribs with more sauce halfway through cooking.

4_ Remove the tray from the oven and put the grill on to high. Brush the ribs once again with the remaining sauce, then grill for 2–3 minutes until the sauce is sticky and is just beginning to char at the edges. Scatter over the spring onions and serve.

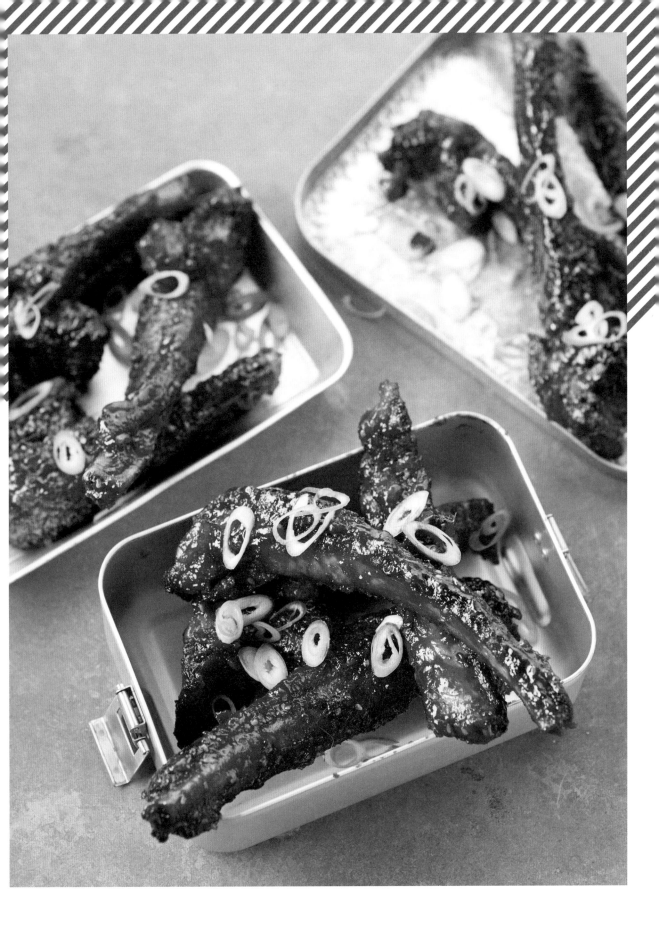

Jeyuk Bokkeum SWEET AND SPICY PORK BELLY BUNS

We sell this classic Korean spicy stir-fried pork dish on our trailer but make a few small changes to turn it into street food. Firstly we cut the pork much finer, into thin matchsticks, so that the fat melts away and it's easier to eat from a bread bun. We also remove the veg, so that the bun is all about the pork, and then we top each bun with a good handful of Mooli Slaw (see page 70).

SERVES
6

1kg (2lb 4oz) pork belly, cut into 5-mm (½-inch) slices
1 tablespoon vegetable oil
1 carrot, thinly sliced
¼ white cabbage, thinly sliced
½ onion, thinly sliced

MARINADE
280g (10oz) *gochujang* (Korean red chilli paste)
6 garlic cloves, minced
1-cm (½-inch) piece of fresh root ginger, peeled and very finely chopped

4 teaspoons sesame oil
270g (9¾oz) golden caster sugar
6 tablespoons regular soy sauce

TO SERVE
6 white burger buns, halved

1_ For the marinade, mix together the *gochujang*, garlic, ginger, sesame oil and sugar in a large bowl, then stir in the soy sauce to loosen and thin the mixture out.

2_ Cut the pork belly slices into pieces approximately 10cm (4 inches) long,

3_ Add the pork pieces to the marinade bowl and mix together with your hands to ensure they are evenly coated in the marinade (it may be easiest to do this a little at a time).

4_ Heat the vegetable oil in a large frying pan over a high heat, add the carrot, cabbage and onion and cook, stirring, for 3–4 minutes until softened. Reduce the heat to medium, then add the pork and marinade mixture to the pan. Cook, stirring continuously to prevent the marinade from catching on the bottom of the pan, for 15–20 minutes or until the pork is cooked through. Share between the burger buns and serve immediately.

Twice-Cooked Crispy Pork Belly

This recipe makes the ultimate Sunday roast – think juicy, tender meat, lightly flavoured with *doenjang* and honey, alongside loads of crispy, crunchy crackling. It works brilliantly eaten wrapped inside a lettuce leaf, Korean-style, or (Gareth's favourite) piled on top of creamy mash with lots of Zingy Green Sauce (see page 79). Whichever way you choose, it's a real crowd-pleaser.

SERVES
4–6

---

1 x 1kg (2lb 4oz) pork belly piece
1 tablespoon vegetable oil
1 tablespoon salt

STOCK
150g (5½oz) fresh root ginger, roughly sliced
10 whole garlic cloves
2 tablespoons light soy sauce

2 tablespoons *doenjang* (Korean soybean paste)
2 long red chillies, trimmed and sliced in half lengthways
1 onion
1 tablespoon black peppercorns

MARINADE
1½ tablespoons *doenjang* (Korean soybean paste)
8 garlic cloves, minced

1-cm (½-inch) piece of fresh root ginger, peeled and very finely chopped
1½ tablespoons honey
1 tablespoon apple vinegar

1_ Put the pork belly piece in a large heavy-based saucepan or stockpot with all the stock ingredients and enough water to cover. Bring to the boil and simmer for 30 minutes, then remove the pork from the stock and leave to drain. Pat dry thoroughly with kitchen paper.

2_ Using the tip of a sharp knife score the skin of the pork belly in a crisscross pattern, being careful not to cut through to the meat. Transfer to the refrigerator and leave for 4–6 hours or preferably overnight to rest.

3_ When ready to cook, preheat the oven to 220°C (425°F), Gas Mark 7.

4_ Mix together the marinade ingredients in a small bowl. Place the pork belly skin-side up on a large sheet of aluminium foil and, using a pastry brush, coat the sides and the bottom of the meat only with marinade (be careful not to get any on the skin as it burns easily). Mix the vegetable oil and salt together in a small bowl and brush over the skin.

5_ Fold the aluminium foil around the pork belly to cover the marinated sides, leaving the skin uncovered. Place in the oven on the highest shelf and roast for 30 minutes, then reduce the heat to 180°C (350°F), Gas Mark 4 and roast for a further 30 minutes.

6_ To make really crispy crackling, the pork needs a final blast of heat, so turn the temperature back up to 220°C (425°F), Gas Mark 7 and cook for 40 minutes more, until the skin is golden brown and crunchy all the way through.

7_ Remove the pork from the oven and leave to rest for 30 minutes before serving.

Gochujang Meatloaf

I'm a little ashamed to admit that the first time we made this meatloaf, I ate it almost in its entirety, all by myself. It's one of those dishes that is incredibly versatile and can be enjoyed either hot or cold, while the mix also makes great meatballs or sausages too. My favourite way to eat it is straight out of the refrigerator, cut into thick slices with a pile of our Mustard Pickled Onions (see page 76), though it is also great seared quickly in a pan for crispy edges, then eaten in a bread bun with a runny fried egg. Make it on a weekend and you've got breakfast, lunch and dinner sorted for the next few days.

SERVES 6

500g (1lb 2oz) minced pork
3 spring onions, trimmed and finely chopped
6 garlic cloves, minced
1 teaspoon salt
1½ tablespoons *gochujang* (Korean red chilli paste)
pinch of pepper

50g (1¾oz) fresh breadcrumbs
½ onion, finely chopped
1 egg

GLAZE
1½ tablespoons apricot jam

1 tablespoon *gochujang* (Korean red chilli paste)
½ tablespoon honey
1 teaspoon regular soy sauce
1 garlic clove, minced
¼ teaspoon sesame oil
½ tablespoon apple vinegar

1_ Preheat the oven to 180°C (350°F), Gas Mark 4. Grease a 450g (1lb) loaf tin.

2_ For the glaze, mix together all the ingredients in a small bowl. Set aside.

3_ Put all the meatloaf ingredients in a large bowl, then stir together with a wooden spoon until well combined. Tip the meatloaf mix into the loaf tin, pressing it down into the corners and using a knife to smooth out and even the top. Bake for 45 minutes, until the meatloaf starts to shrink from the edges of the tin.

4_ Remove the meatloaf from the oven and, using a skewer, poke holes all over the top. Pour over the glaze (this will sink into and flavour the meat as well as forming a lovely topping) and put it back in the oven for a further 20 minutes, until the glaze becomes nice and sticky. Serve hot or cold (this will keep in the fridge, covered, for 3 days.

Kimchi Wang Mandu _KIMCHI AND PORK STEAMED BUNS_

There's something a little magical about watching steamed buns being made in the market – the way that they're hidden from sight until they're just cooked, and then revealed in clouds of billowing steam as the lids are lifted from the steamers. These buns can be filled with anything, sweet or savoury, although _kimchi_ and pork has always been my favourite choice as the salty, spicy filling is the perfect contrast to the plain, soft, pillowy buns.

MAKES
8
BUNS

vegetable oil, for greasing

DOUGH
250ml (9fl oz) warm water
2½ teaspoons active dried yeast
3 tablespoons caster sugar
420g (15oz) plain flour
1½ teaspoons baking powder

FILLING
40g (1½oz) dangmyeon sweet potato noodles
1 tablespoon vegetable oil
300g (10½oz) minced pork
pinch of salt
pinch of pepper
150g (5½oz) matured _Baechu Kimchi_
 (see page 32), drained and finely chopped

1 garlic clove, minced
2 spring onions, trimmed and finely chopped
1 long red chilli, trimmed and finely chopped
1 tablespoon regular soy sauce
170g (6oz) firm tofu

1_ To make the dough, in a small bowl, stir together the water, yeast and 1 tablespoon of the sugar. Set aside for 10 minutes to allow the yeast to activate.

2_ In a large bowl, mix together the flour, baking powder, salt and remaining 2 tablespoons of sugar. Slowly add the yeast mixture to the bowl and stir together with a wooden spoon to form a dough.

3_ Tip the dough out onto a lightly floured surface and knead for 10 minutes until smooth and elastic. Brush the inside of a mixing bowl with oil and add the dough. Brush the dough lightly with oil, cover loosely with clingfilm and leave in a warm place for 1 hour to prove until doubled in size.

4_ While the dough is proving, make the filling. Soak the sweet potato noodles in enough boiling water to cover for 10 minutes. Drain and rinse under cold water to cool, then cut into 5-mm (¼-inch) lengths. Heat the vegetable oil in a large frying pan over a medium-high heat, add the minced pork and fry for 2–3 minutes, stirring occasionally, until browned all over. Add the salt, pepper, _kimchi_ and garlic to the pan, cook for 2 minutes more, then add the spring onions, chilli and soy sauce. Crumble over the tofu and cook for a further 2 minutes, using the back of a wooden spoon to break up any large lumps of tofu, then add the sweet potato noodles and mix everything together well. Set aside to cool.

5_ Once proved, gently tip the risen dough onto a lightly floured surface and knead for 5 minutes to knock back

any air bubbles. Brush the inside of the bowl with some more oil and return the dough to the bowl, then brush the top of the dough with a little more oil and cover it again loosely with clingfilm. Leave to prove for another 15 minutes.

6_ Once the dough has proved for the second time, tip it back onto the floured surface and knead for 5 minutes to loosen it up again. Shape the dough into a long sausage, then divide it into eight equal-sized pieces. Roll each piece out into a thin circle about 12cm (4½ inches) in diameter.

7_ Flour your hands and take a piece of dough so it lies flat across your palm. Place 2–3 tablespoons of your cooled filling into the middle of the dough, then pull one edge of your dough to the centre and brush the outside edge with water. Continue pulling the edges of the dough into the centre, working around your bun, dabbing it with a little more water each time to stick the dough down. Once all the edges are at the centre, twist the middle of the bun to seal.

8_ Cut a sheet of greaseproof paper into eight 7-cm (2¾-inch) squares and brush each with a little vegetable oil. Lay these on the base of a bamboo or metal steamer, then place a bun (seal-side up) on top of each square, ensuring there is plenty of room between them to allow for expansion while cooking. Steam for 15 minutes, then turn off the heat, remove the lid and leave to stand for 5 minutes to allow the excess steam to dissipate.

Serve with _Cho Ganjang_ (see page 21) for dipping.

O-ri Bulgogi SPICY SHARING DUCK WITH FRIED RICE

This dish will always be pretty special to us. We were introduced to it on Gareth's first trip to Busan by my uncle. We were in a restaurant, sitting on the floor, on low tables with the duck simmering in a huge dish in the middle of the table. My family is pretty loud when we all get together, so Gareth was just sitting eating, taking in the cacophony of noise around him, when all of sudden and much to his surprise, his bowl of rice was whisked away from him. In fact, all the rice bowls around the table were collected and thrown into the remaining duck sauce, along with a handful of dried seaweed. The little bits of leftover duck, the sauce, rice and seaweed were all fried together until the rice began to catch and become a little crispy, before being served back in the original rice bowls. This is the best part of this dish — the rice soaks up all the flavours from the duck and also gets a slightly smoky flavour, as the sauce begins to catch — it'll be the best fried rice you'll ever have and it's the reason that *O-ri Bulgogi* became Gareth's favourite Korean dish.

SERVES
4

450g (1lb) skin-on duck breast, cut into 5-mm (¼-inch) thick slices
1 onion, finely sliced
1 tablespoon vegetable oil
30g (1oz) chives, roughly chopped
200g (7oz) cooked short-grain rice (see page 26), plus extra to serve

1 tablespoon sesame oil
2 dried *gim* (nori) seaweed sheets, sliced into fine matchsticks
2 spring onions, trimmed and finely sliced

MARINADE
12 garlic cloves, minced
3 tablespoons *gochujang* (Korean red chilli paste)
1 tablespoon *gochugaru* (Korean red chilli powder)
2 tablespoons apricot jam or *maesil* (Korean plum extract)
3 tablespoons regular soy sauce
1 teaspoon sesame oil

1_ Mix the marinade ingredients together in a large bowl. Add the duck slices and onion to the bowl and mix together well so that everything is evenly coated in the marinade. Cover with clingfilm, transfer to the refrigerator and leave to marinate for at least 2 hours, preferably overnight.

2_ When you are ready to cook, pour the vegetable oil into a heavy-based frying pan over a medium heat. Add the marinated duck mixture to the pan, and fry for 4 minutes, stirring and turning the duck pieces as you go, until the duck is just cooked through and the sauce has reduced slightly and become sticky. Stir through the chives until just wilted, then transfer the still-sizzling pan to a heatproof stand in the middle of the table. Serve with rice.

3_ Once you have worked your way through most of the duck and are left with the sticky remains of the sauce and just a few small pieces in the pan, return it to the stove over a medium heat. Add the rice, sesame oil, seaweed and spring onions, stir everything together well, then press the mix against the bottom of the pan with the back of a wooden spoon to create an even layer. Leave for 2–3 minutes to crisp (and catch a little) on the bottom, then return the pan to the table and enjoy.

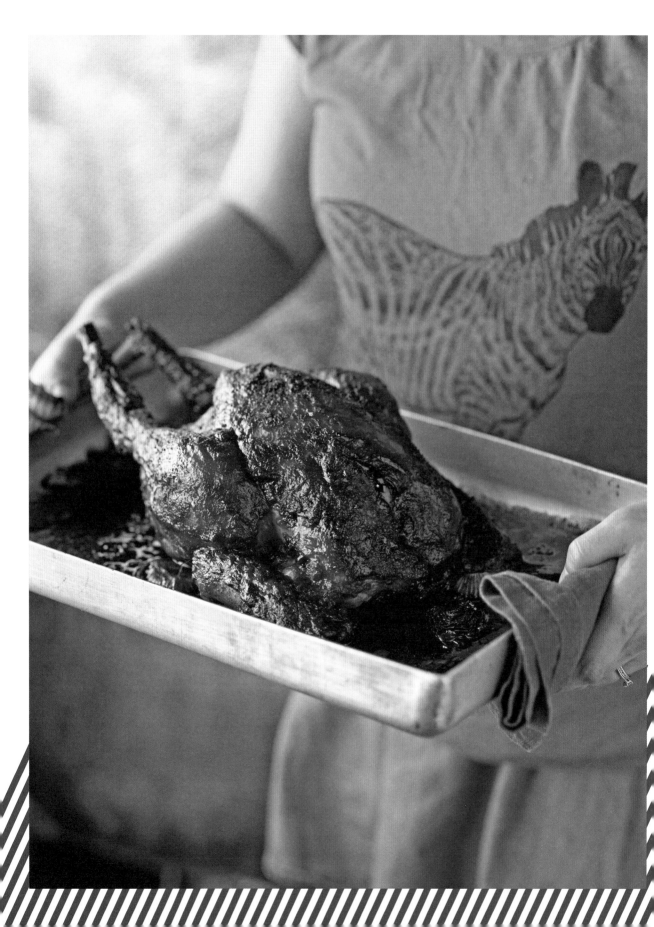

Sticky Ginger Roast Chicken

When I think of this roast chicken, I always picture it as a real weekend treat, but it's so simple you could really just as easily have it as a mid-week dinner. Just remember to marinate it and leave it in the refrigerator the night before to keep things quick. You'll be rewarded with super-juicy chicken, slippery sweet onions and a spicy ginger sauce — all you'll need to finish it will be a simple bowl of steamed rice or veg. Workdays can feel long, so it's nice to know you'll have something delicious for dinner, just waiting to be popped in the oven when you get home.

SERVES
4

2 onions
1 whole chicken, about 1.5kg (3lb 5oz)
50g (1¾oz) fresh root ginger, roughly sliced
4 whole garlic cloves
2 spring onions, trimmed and cut into thirds

MARINADE
5 tablespoons *gochujang* (Korean red chilli paste)
1-cm (½-inch) piece of fresh root ginger, peeled and very finely chopped
6 garlic cloves, minced

150ml (¼ pint) ginger beer
2 tablespoons clear runny honey
2 tablespoons light soy sauce
½ tablespoon salt

1_ Combine all the marinade ingredients in a small bowl. Slice the onions into 1-cm (½-inch) rounds and lay them on the bottom of a roasting tin.

2_ Loosely stuff the cavity of the chicken with the ginger slices, garlic cloves and spring onions. Place the chicken in a large roasting tray and pour over half the marinade to cover, making sure to rub it into the creases of the wings and legs as well as the underside of the chicken. Then place the chicken into the roasting tin with the onions and transfer to the refrigerator to marinate for at least 1 hour.

3_ When you are ready to cook, preheat the oven to 190°C (375°F), Gas Mark 5. Place the chicken tray on the middle shelf and roast for 1¼ hours, brushing it with a little of the remaining marinade every 10 minutes or so.

4_ Remove the chicken from the oven and pour over any leftover marinade. Turn the oven up to 220°C (425°F), Gas Mark 7, return the chicken to the oven and roast for a further 10–15 minutes, until the skin is nicely golden and sticky and the chicken is cooked through (if it looks like it might be getting a bit too brown at any point, cover it loosely with aluminium foil and continue cooking).

5_ Leave the chicken to rest for half an hour before carving. Serve with the onions, spooning a little of the sweet juices from the bottom of the roasting tin over each portion.

Ramyun Chicken Buns

Using instant noodles here to create a coating for the fried chicken not only gives these buns extra crunch, it also helps to lock in all that moisture. The result is really juicy, crispy chicken that's the perfect contrast to a soft bread bun. I've eaten the *Shin* brand of *Ramyun* instant noodles — which is known for being pretty spicy — for as long as I can remember. A few Koreans I know call the little sachet of spice mix they come with 'magic dust', and add it to their cooking of other dishes for an extra kick. If you're a chilli lover, sprinkle a little of it over the cooked chicken thighs for extra heat when serving.

SERVES
6

6 boneless, skinless chicken thighs
1 litre (1¾ pints) *Kimchi* Brine (see page 94)
2 x 120g (4½oz) *ramyun* Korean instant noodle packets
2 eggs
vegetable oil, for deep-frying

TO SERVE
6 burger buns
¼ iceberg lettuce, shredded
6 tablespoons mayonnaise, either shop-bought or
    homemade (see page 83)
6 tablespoons Korean Sweet Chilli Sauce (see page 86)

1_ Put the chicken thighs in a large bowl and pour over the brine. Transfer to the refrigerator and leave to brine for 1 hour.

2_ After 1 hour, drain the chicken thighs and rinse them under cold running water to remove the excess salt from the brine, then pat dry with kitchen paper.

3_ Break the instant noodles into small chunks and put in a food processor. Pulse until the noodles are fully broken down and are a similar size to breadcrumbs, then tip the noodle 'crumbs' onto a large plate. Crack the eggs into a small bowl and whisk together.

4_ Half-fill a large saucepan or deep-fryer with vegetable oil and preheat to 180°C (350°F), or until a cube of bread browns in 30 seconds.

5_ Dip a chicken thigh first in the egg and then in the noodle 'crumbs', ensuring it is completed coated. Shake off any excess noodle coating, then repeat with the remaining thighs.

6_ Lower the chicken thighs carefully into the hot oil and cook for 6–7 minutes. Lift the chicken out of the oil and leave to rest for 5 minutes, then carefully lower back into the oil and fry for a further 3–4 minutes, until the noodle coating is golden brown and crunchy. Drain the chicken on kitchen paper to get rid of the excess oil.

7_ Slice the buns in half and lay them cut-side down in a large dry frying pan over a high heat, for 30–40 seconds, until warmed through and slightly charred at the edges.

8_ To assemble, arrange the shredded lettuce on the bottom bun halves. Spoon over the mayo, then top each bun half with a chicken thigh. Dollop over the chilli sauce, sandwich together with the bun lid and enjoy in big, messy mouthfuls.

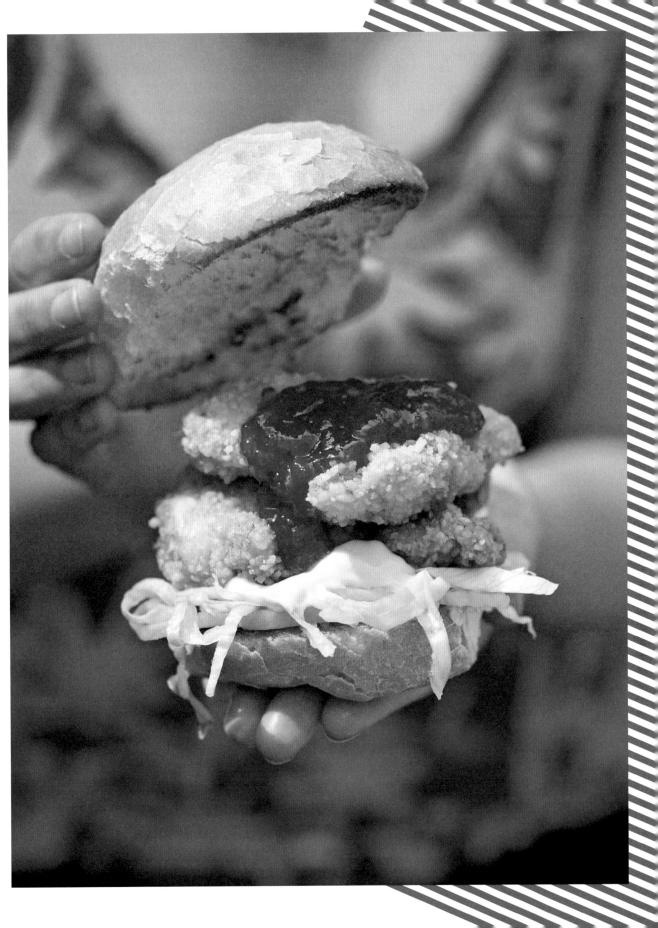

Pomegranate-glazed Lamb Kebabs

Kebabs have become increasingly popular in Seoul. We'd noticed a few kebab shops popping up in the expat district of Itaewon some years back and now, as street food, kebabs have started to make their way into mainstream areas such as Myeong Dong too. This isn't much of surprise – as kebabs are essentially just grilled meats they work really well with all the typical Korean accompaniments. The pomegranate juice here gives this marinade a tart fruitiness, while the mango *kimchi* brings a really nice sweetness to the lamb. It's the kind of messy food that feels like it should be really bad for you, though as fast food goes, it's actually a pretty healthy option.

MAKES 4

625g (1lb 6oz) boneless lamb leg, cut into 3-cm (1¼-inch) cubes
4 spring onions, trimmed and cut into thirds
1 red pepper, cored, deseeded and cut into 3-cm (1¼-inch) cubes
12 garlic cloves, minced
4 tablespoons regular soy sauce

125ml pomegranate juice
4 tablespoons clear runny honey
2 teaspoons apple vinegar
1 tablespoon vegetable oil

4 bamboo skewers, soaked in water for at least 10 minutes

TO SERVE
4 pitta breads
¼ iceberg lettuce, shredded
125g (4½oz) Mango *Kimchi* (see page 38)
250ml (9fl oz) natural yogurt

1_ Mix all the ingredients except the vegetable oil together in a large bowl, cover with clingfilm and leave in the refrigerator to marinate for at least 30 minutes.

2_ When you are ready to cook, thread the pepper, lamb and spring onion pieces onto the skewers in an alternating pattern, leaving about 5cm (2 inches) empty at either end (this will give you something to hold onto as you turn them during cooking). Set the remaining marinade to one side.

3_ Brush a cast-iron griddle pan with the vegetable oil and place over a medium-high heat.

4_ Carefully lay the kebabs on the griddle and cook for 3–4 minutes on each of the four sides, brushing occasionally with the marinade, until the lamb is nicely browned and cooked to your liking. Remove from the heat and set aside for 2 minutes to rest.

5_ While the kebabs are resting, add the pitta breads to the pan to heat through for 30 seconds on each side.

6_ To serve, split the pitta breads open and stuff each with a handful of lettuce. Slide the kebab pieces off the skewers and pile into the pitta breads along with the mango *kimchi* and yogurt.

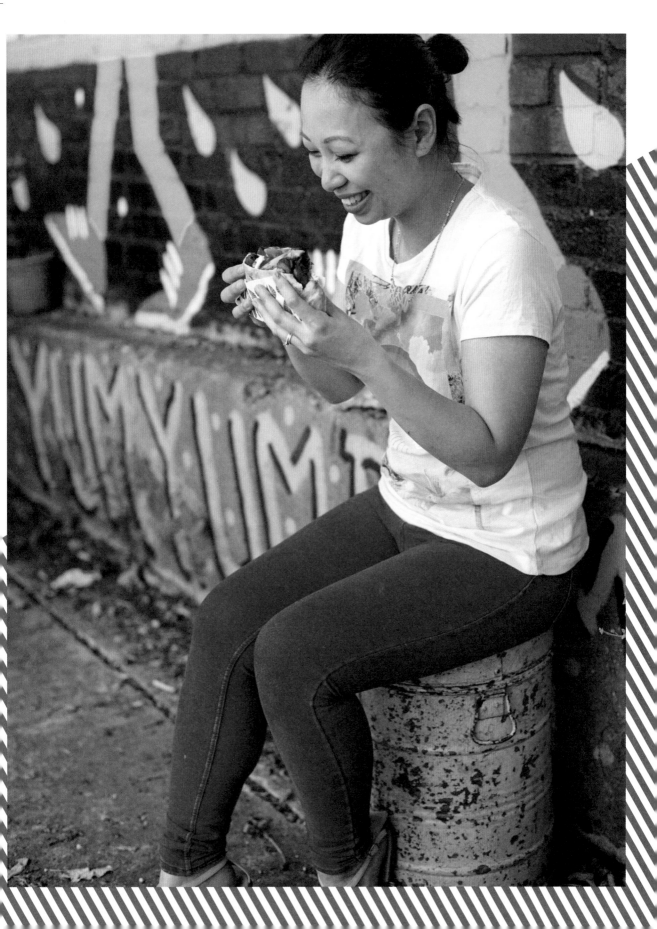

Go Galbi GRILLED MACKEREL

Translating as 'mackerel ribs', this is a typical Busan dish, where the mackerel goes really crispy, so you can pick the fish up by the spines and eat the flesh as you would a meat rib. Though not for the faint-hearted, when the bones are really crispy like this you can even eat them whole.

SERVES 2

1 mackerel, about 375g (13oz)
pinch of salt
2 tablespoons *Yangnyum Jang* (see page 21), to serve

1_ Cut along the belly of the mackerel with a sharp knife or scissors, remove the guts and wash the cavity clean. Remove the head and fins.

2_ Working from the inside of the mackerel belly, run a knife down either side of the spine until you reach the tail, then pull the fish open like the pages of a book, keeping the spine intact.

3_ Cover a large baking sheet with aluminium foil and preheat the grill to high.

4_ Place the mackerel on the foil skin-side down and sprinkle over the salt. Grill for 5 minutes, then flip the mackerel over and grill flesh-side down for a further 5 minutes until the skin is browned and the fish is cooked through.

5_ Transfer to a large plate and serve with the *yangnyum jang* spooned over.

Korean Chilli Crab

My family have been going to Jin Go Gae, a Korean restaurant in south-west London's New Malden, for the past five or six years. It's not particularly conveniently located and it's pretty far from any station, but it's always full, as it's known to be one of the best and most authentic Korean restaurants around. In fact, my parents still travel up from Portsmouth to visit it almost every month. One of my favourite dishes there is a spicy marinated raw crab dish called *yangnyum gejang* – in Korea, this dish is nicknamed 'the rice thief,' because the sauce is so good that you keep going back for more rice to mop it up. Though I love it, raw crab isn't for everyone, so this is our version. It's addictive, messy and delicious.

SERVES
2

1 large whole brown crab, or 2 small crabs, about 1.5kg (3lb 5oz) in total
100g (3½oz) cooked short-grain rice (see page 26)
2 spring onions, trimmed and thinly sliced, to garnish

SAUCE
2 tablespoons regular soy sauce
4 tablespoons *gochugaru* (Korean red chilli powder)
1 tablespoon corn syrup
5-mm (¼-inch) piece of fresh root ginger, peeled and very finely chopped
1 tablespoon sesame oil

1 tablespoon mirin
4 garlic cloves, minced
1 tablespoon fish sauce
1 tablespoon apricot jam
1 tablespoon white rice vinegar
1 tablespoon roasted sesame seeds

1_ If you're cooking a live crab, put it in the freezer for 20 minutes to numb it prior to cooking.

2_ Fill a large pot with water and bring it to a vigorous boil. Lower in the crab, making sure that it is fully submerged and cook for 12 minutes. Remove the crab from the water and set aside to cool.

3_ While the crab is cooling, make the sauce by mixing together all the ingredients in a bowl.

4_ Once the crab is cooled, remove the legs and claws by gently twisting them off from where they meet the body. Set aside 3 tablespoons of the sauce and put the remaining sauce in a large bowl. Crack each of the legs and claws with a nutcracker or by hitting them swiftly with a large knife and then put these into the bowl with the sauce.

5_ Lay the crab on its back and carefully push a knife between the shell and central body part or 'purse' of the crab to prise it open. Set the purse aside. Drain away any water left in the shell, then remove and discard the circle of grey feathery gills ('dead man's fingers').

6_ Using a teaspoon, scoop out the remaining brown crabmeat from the inside of the shell and spoon it into a small bowl. Mash the crabmeat with a fork, add the rice and the remaining sauce and mix together thoroughly. Set aside.

7_ Rinse the shell out under running water and dry thoroughly.

8_ Cut the crab purse into quarters using a large knife. Pick out the white crabmeat and put it in a small bowl.

9_ Lay the cleaned shell on a serving dish and fill it with the brown crabmeat and rice mix. Spoon over the white crabmeat and garnish with the spring onions.

10_ Pile the spicy claws and legs around the dressed crab and serve. Be sure to eat this with plenty of napkins – it's a messy one.

Ojingeo Bokkeum STIR-FRIED SPICY SQUID

With its addictively spicy sauce and tender, soft squid, *ojingeo bokkeum* is one of Korea's most popular squid dishes. It can be found on the menus of snack houses, served as a simple lunch with a side of rice, or in the middle of the table to share as a *banchan*.

SERVES
2

1 whole squid, about 175g (6oz), cleaned and quill removed (ask the fishmonger to do this for you)
1 tablespoon vegetable oil
1 onion, finely sliced
½ carrot, cut into thin diagonal strips
1 spring onion, trimmed and roughly chopped

1 long red chilli, trimmed and roughly chopped
1 teaspoon roasted sesame seeds, to garnish

SAUCE
1 tablespoon *gochujang* (Korean red chilli paste)
2 tablespoons *gochugaru* (Korean red chilli powder)

3 garlic cloves, minced
1 tablespoon mirin
1 tablespoon regular soy sauce
1 tablespoon caster sugar
2 tablespoons water, plus extra if needed

1_ Slice the squid tube open to lay it flat, then run the tip of your knife along the squid lightly in a diagonal criss-cross pattern (this will help the squid curl up nicely while cooking). Cut the squid into 2.5-cm (1-inch) squares.

2_ For the sauce, mix all the ingredients together in a bowl.

3_ Heat the oil in a frying pan over a medium heat. Add the onion and carrot and fry for 3–4 minutes, stirring occasionally, until softened.

4_ Add the squid, spring onion, chilli and sauce to the pan. Fry for 2–3 minutes, stirring, until the squid is tender and cooked through, adding another tablespoon or two of water if the sauce looks like it is getting too sticky and reduced. Scatter over the sesame seeds and serve.

Prawn Po' Boy with Yuja Mayo

Gareth had always wanted to add a take on a po' boy to our menu as he's a big fan of this style of American sandwich, but it took us a while to decide on the filling. The breakthrough came when we were hosting a pop-up one summer at Old Bengal Bar in East London and were able to dedicate some time to testing lots of different ideas. Stuffed full of juicy prawns, fresh crispy lettuce and lots of bright, citrussy mayo, this is Gareth's idea of the perfect sandwich.

SERVES
6

24 large raw whole prawns, about 650g (1lb 7oz)
vegetable oil, for deep-frying
4 hoagie or firm submarine rolls
½ iceberg lettuce, shredded
2 tomatoes, thinly sliced

YUJA MAYO
2 egg yolks
¼ teaspoon English mustard

1 tablespoon *yuja* (yuzu) juice
2 teaspoons lemon juice
pinch of salt
½ tablespoon apple vinegar
100ml (3½fl oz) vegetable oil

COATING
60g (2¼oz) self-raising flour
80g (3oz) potato starch

40g (1½oz) cornmeal
pinch of salt
1 teaspoon baking powder
¼ teaspoon garlic granules
2 tablespoons *gochugaru* (Korean red chilli powder)

1_ For the *yuja* mayo, put the egg yolks, mustard, *yuja* juice, lemon juice, salt and apple vinegar in a food processor and blend together. With the motor running, pour in the vegetable oil in a thin, stready stream until you have a thick, creamy mayonnaise. Set aside.

2_ Peel the prawns and remove the heads. Using a small, sharp knife, make a shallow cut along the back of each prawn, then lift out the dark vein with the tip of a knife. Rinse under cold running water and drain.

3_ Half-fill a large pot or deep-fryer with vegetable oil and preheat to 180°C (350°F), or until a cube of bread browns in 30 seconds.

4_ Mix all the coating ingredients together in a large bowl. Add the prawns and toss together to ensure they are thoroughly coated, then lower them gently into the hot oil and fry for 1½ minutes. Remove the prawns from the oil, season with salt and leave to drain on kitchen paper.

5_ Slice the bread rolls open and slather with the mayo, then pile in the lettuce, tomato and prawns. Enjoy.

California Rolls

While now I'm a complete convert, I'd never been that big a fan of California rolls – and definitely never really considered them particularly Korean – until I started working at Korea Foods. There the girls in the office would almost always eat lunch together and, on special occasions, we'd always have California rolls. Mrs Kim (the mother hen of the group), would make sure to organize it the day before and everyone would bring in one of the roll elements, then on roll day itself all the different ingredients would be heaped in piles in the middle of the table, and everyone would dive in and make their own. I loved how everyone could assemble the rolls to their own tastes and, most importantly, how this great sharing dish really brought everyone together.

SERVES 8

4 eggs
pinch of salt
½ tablespoon vegetable oil
250g (9oz) seafood sticks

4 teaspoons wasabi (or English mustard)
8 tablespoons mayonnaise, either shop-bought or homemade (see page 83)
1kg (2lb 4oz) cooked short-grain rice (see page 26)

2 red peppers, cored, deseeded and finely sliced
4 ripe avocados, stoned and sliced lengthways
24 dried *gim* (nori) seaweed sheets, cut into quarters
250ml (9fl oz) regular soy sauce, to serve

1_ Whisk together the eggs with the salt in a bowl.

2_ Heat the vegetable oil in a heavy-based frying pan over a medium heat and pour in half the egg mix. Tip the pan so that the eggs are spread evenly to create a large, thin omelette, then fry for 30 seconds on each side. Remove the omelette from the pan and set aside to cool, then repeat with the remaining beaten egg to create a second omelette. Once cool, slice the omelettes into 1-cm (½-inch) thick strips.

3_ Shred the seafood sticks into fine strands, put in a bowl with the wasabi and mayonnaise and mix everything together well.

4_ Tip the rice into a large bowl. Arrange the omelette slices, seafood stick mix and all the other ingredients on a large tray and serve in the middle of the table alongside the rice for everyone to assemble their own rolls. To make one, lay a seaweed quarter in the palm of your hand and spread a tablespoon or so of the rice in the middle, then arrange any combination of your assembled ingredients on top. Roll up, dip in the soy sauce and enjoy!

TIP: I've only listed my favourite fillings here, though you can really add whatever you like – cucumbers, stir-fried *eomuk* (Korean fishcakes), tinned tuna and pickled mooli were all popular fillings on California roll day. If you're not a fan of avocado (I'm not), I'd really encourage you to try it here anyway – it gives the rolls a really great creamy texture and with all the other flavours, you won't really taste it in any case.

Soups & Stews

YOU
SCRATCH
WHERE
IT ITCHES

Soups and stews are the comfort food of Korea. Ask any Korean person what their favourite Korean food is and most of them will reply either doenjang jjigae or kimchi jjigae. These stews are often cooked at home rather than eaten in restaurants, and so many people have memories associated with eating these growing up.

Though Korea might be best known for its barbecue, it's the soups and stews which provide the backbone of a Korean meal. Traditionally meat was expensive in Korea, so big barbecues were reserved for special occasions and for eating out. Instead, a Korean home-cooked meal would normally consist of individual bowls of rice, a selection of *banchan* and, almost always, some sort of soup or stew.

Salt is rarely used as a seasoning, instead soups and stews are usually flavoured with the Korean *jang* ingredients of *ganjang* (soy sauce), *gochujang* (Korean red chilli paste) and *doenjang* (Korean soybean paste). It's also important to use a good stock such as the anchovy stock *Myeulchi Gookmul* (see page 22) as the base, as this gives the soups and stews plenty of depth.

There are so many different soups and stews available in Korea that we've only been able to include our absolute favourites in this book. They can be split into the following types:

Guk
Guk, pronounced 'gook' are usually simple soups that are often only simmered for a short period of time. These soups are typically very light and can be served as palate cleansers, and include examples such as *Jo-Gae Guk* (see page 154), which is often served alongside spicy dishes to cool the mouth down.

Tang
Tangs are thicker, slightly heavier soups. They are usually more substantial than *guks* because they'll often contain chunks of meat or fish and include examples such as *Mae-Un-Tang* (see page 148) and *Dak Bokkeum Tang* (see page 144).

Jjigae
Korean stews, *jjigae* are pure comfort food for a lot of Koreans as they encompass the family favourites of *Kimchi Jjigae* (see page 138) and *Doenjang Jjigae* (see page 141). *Jjigae* are often served in hot stone bowls to preserve their heat, so that they arrive at the table still bubbling.

Jorim
Jorim refer to braised dishes such as *Godeungeo Jorim* (see page 152) where the meat or fish is the star of the show. These are usually served in a big dish in the middle of the table for everyone to share.

Jjim
Jjim refers to steaming or boiling in a flavoured sauce or soup, often cooked in a pressure cooker in a Korea. The liquid in *jjims* such as *Mae-Un Jjim Dak* (see page 144) is usually then simmered down to reduce it to a thicker sauce to coat all the ingredients.

Kimchi Jjigae KIMCHI STEW

I'm always torn between whether this or *Doenjang Jjigae* (see page 141) is my favourite Korean dish. Both are real home-cooking comfort foods and are so easy to put together – in fact, I think this was the first Korean dish that my mum ever taught me to make. The recipe is really simple, but there are a few key elements to a great *kimchi jjigae*. Firstly, your *kimchi* must be very mature and fermented, almost vinegary and super-tangy – a young kimchi won't flavour the broth enough, and you'll be left with a very watery dish. Secondly, it's essential that you fry the *kimchi* for at least 10 minutes to bring out all its flavours and make this stew as rich and spicy as it can be. Thirdly, don't chop the *kimchi* too finely, as you want to make sure it will still have a nice crunch.

SERVES 4

1 tablespoon vegetable oil
750g (1lb 10oz) extra-mature *Baechu Kimchi* (see page 32), roughly chopped
200g (7oz) pork belly, finely sliced

1 litre (1¾ pints) water
250g (9oz) firm tofu, cut into 5-cm (2-inch) squares
1 spring onion, trimmed and sliced at an angle, to garnish

1_ Heat the oil in a large heavy-based saucepan or stockpot over a medium heat.

2_ Take the *kimchi* out of its fermenting 'juice', add to the pan and fry for 10 minutes, stirring occasionally. Add the pork belly and 2–3 tablespoons of the *kimchi* juice to the pan and fry for a further 5 minutes until the pork is browned and the liquid has evaporated.

3_ Pour the measurement water into the pan, bring to a simmer and leave to cook, uncovered, for 30 minutes until reduced down. Lay the tofu squares evenly over the top of the stew, cover with a lid and simmer for 3–4 minutes, until the tofu is heated through. Ladle into bowls and serve scattered with the spring onion to garnish.

TIPS: The *kimchi* I use here is usually one that I've had in the refrigerator for so long that it's almost fizzy with sour, fermented flavours, but if you're using shop-bought *kimchi* or your *kimchi* has only matured for a few weeks, add half a chicken stock cube in with the *kimchi* as you fry it for extra flavour.

On days when I don't have pork belly in the house, I just drain a tin of tuna and use this instead (add this just before the tofu, as it'll break up too much if you stew it for too long). Tuna is a popular substitute for meat here – in Korea, you can even get 'tuna for *kimchi jjigae*', which sometimes even comes in meat-shaped cubes!

Budae Jjigae ARMY BASE STEW

During the Korean War, food was scarce and meat in particular was considered a real luxury. When American soldiers brought Spam over to Korea in their ration packs, Koreans started cooking with it — along with other ingredients such as hot-dogs and processed cheese — and created this hot, spicy stew. While the combination of instant noodles, Spam, hot-dogs and processed cheese might sound like the inside of a student's cupboard, they actually make a really hearty, warming meal. Last summer, I was lucky enough to be invited onto a BBC show to cook *Buddae Jjigae* for our Marines, to show them that the Spam in their ration packs actually had the potential to taste good! Most of them were surprisingly won over — it's a lot tastier than it sounds.

SERVES
4

1 tablespoon vegetable oil
100g (3½oz) Spam, sliced into thin squares
2 hot-dogs, finely sliced
1 litre (1¾ pints) *Myeulchi Gookmul* (see page 22)
2 spring onions, trimmed and finely sliced
100g minced pork
100g (3½oz) *Baechu Kimchi* (see page 32), roughly chopped

100g (3½oz) rice cake discs for soup (optional)
1 x 120g (4½oz) *ramyun* Korean instant noodle packet
2–3 processed cheese slices

SAUCE
2 tablespoons *gochugaru* (Korean red chilli powder)
1 tablespoon *gochujang* (Korean red chilli paste)
1 tablespoon light soy sauce

4 garlic cloves, minced
1 teaspoon caster sugar
pinch of salt
pinch of pepper

1_ For the sauce, mix together all the ingredients in a bowl. Set aside.

2_ Heat the vegetable oil in a large saucepan or stockpot over a medium heat. Add the Spam and hot-dog pieces and fry for 2–3 minutes until the edges begin to brown and crisp up, then pour over the stock and bring to the boil.

3_ Add the sauce, spring onions, minced pork, *kimchi* and rice cakes, if using, to the pan. Reduce the heat to a simmer and cook for 10 minutes, stirring occasionally until the minced pork is cooked through.

4_ Gently lower the noodles onto the top of the simmering stew, being careful not to submerge them in the liquid (this will prevent them from being overcooked). Lay the cheese slices over the noodles and leave to simmer for a further 2 minutes, then transfer the still-bubbling pan to a heatproof stand in the middle of the table or ladle into bowls and serve immediately.

TIP: Korean rice cake discs can be found in either the frozen or chilled section of Asian supermarkets. They don't have a lot of flavour, but have a great chewy texture and are really filling, so can help to make soups stretch a lot further.

Doenjang Jjigae KOREAN SOYBEAN STEW

For most Koreans, this is the ultimate comfort food. It's the dish that they crave when they think of home — and almost every Korean will say that their mum makes the best version they've ever tasted. My mum makes a really good *doenjang jjigae*, but it's actually my aunt who makes the best (sorry Umma!). She eats it for breakfast, lunch and dinner, so she's got it down to a fine art. As Koreans rarely write recipes down and it's often a case of throwing everything in a pot, tasting it and then adjusting it until it's perfect, this is the closest I can get to her version.

SERVES 4

1.25 litres (2 pints) *Myeulchi Gookmul* (see page 22)
200g (7oz) pork belly, finely sliced
½ onion, thinly sliced
½ bird's eye chilli, trimmed and thinly sliced
2 garlic cloves, sliced

½ tablespoon *gochujang* (Korean red chilli paste)
1 tablespoon *gochugaru* (Korean red chilli powder)
3 tablespoons *doenjang* (Korean soybean paste)
1 tablespoon small dried shrimps, optional

½ courgette, halved lengthways and cut into 1-cm (½-inch) slices
200g (7oz) firm tofu, cut into 5-cm (2-inch) squares

1_ Bring the stock to a boil in a large saucepan or stockpot. Add the pork, onion, chilli, garlic, *gochujang*, *gochugaru*, *doenjang* and dried shrimps, if using, and stir together well. Reduce the heat to a simmer and cook for 5 minutes, then add the courgette slices and cook for a further 10–12 minutes, until the courgette has softened.

2_ Lay the tofu squares evenly over the top of the stew, cover with a lid and simmer for 3–4 minutes, until the tofu is heated through. Serve bubbling and steaming hot.

TIP: Feel free to tweak this recipe to your own taste – mushrooms, clams and potatoes are all common additions, although you can really add any veg, meat or seafood you like. Who knows, maybe your version will turn out as good as my aunt's… maybe!

Soondubu Jjigae SPICY SILKEN TOFU STEW

This is my go-to order whenever I go to a Korean restaurant. Spicy, punchy and with a lovely creamy texture from the silken tofu that could change the minds of even the toughest of tofu cynics, it's pretty irresistible. The clams are the magic ingredient here, giving the stew an unbeatable depth of flavour.

SERVES
2
AS A MAIN

150g (5½oz) clams
1 tablespoon salt
1 tablespoon vegetable oil
100g (3½oz) stewing beef
½ onion, thinly sliced
½ courgette, thinly sliced

4–5 fresh shiitake mushrooms, trimmed and finely sliced
2 bird's eye chillies, finely sliced
1 litre (1¾ pints) *Myeulchi Gookmul* (see page 22)
250g (9oz) extra-soft silken tofu
2 eggs
1 spring onion, trimmed and finely sliced, to garnish

SEASONING PASTE
1 teaspoon sesame oil
3 tablespoons *gochugaru* (Korean red chilli powder)
6 garlic cloves, minced
1 tablespoon regular soy sauce

1_ Sort through the clam shells, discarding any that are broken or don't close when tapped gently. Put the remaining clams in a large bowl with the salt and cover with cold water. Cover with aluminium foil, transfer to the refrigerator and leave to soak for 2 hours, then drain and rinse the clams thoroughly under cold running water.

2_ For the seasoning paste, mix together the sesame oil, *gochugaru*, garlic and soy sauce in a bowl.

3_ Heat the vegetable oil in a large saucepan or stockpot over a medium heat. Add the seasoning paste and fry for 2 minutes, making sure to keep stirring as it catches easily, until fragrant. Add the beef and fry for a further 2–3 minutes, stirring, until browned. Stir in the onion, courgette, mushrooms and chillies ensuring everything is evenly coated in the paste, then pour over the stock.

4_ Bring the soup to a boil, reduce the heat to a simmer and cook gently for 5 minutes, until the vegetables have softened. Stir in the tofu and clams and simmer for a further 3–4 minutes, until the clams have opened (discard any that are still shut). Return to the boil, add the eggs and stir through briefly, then remove from the heat. Ladle into bowls, scatter over the spring onions and serve bubbling hot.

Sogogi Gori Jjim BRAISED OXTAIL STEW

We came up with this dish one night when we were planning a Korean feast for some friends. We'd thought of cooking *galbi jjim* (a Korean short rib stew), but when we went to pick up our ingredients, we couldn't resist the big chunks of oxtail at the butcher's counter. Oxtail doesn't have a lot of meat to it, but its centre is filled with bone marrow, which makes this sauce deliciously rich and glossy. Once cooked, the meat will be tender and juicy and will fall off the bone at the lightest touch. On a cold winter's night, you'd be hard-pressed to find a better meal.

SERVES 6

1.2kg (2lb 10oz) oxtail, cut into 5-cm (2-inch) chunks
2½ tablespoons plain flour
pinch of salt
pinch of finely ground white pepper
2 tablespoons vegetable oil
1 onion, finely chopped
2 carrots, finely chopped
1-cm (½-inch) piece of fresh root ginger, peeled and very finely chopped

4 garlic cloves, minced
2 kiwifruit, peeled and finely chopped
1 tablespoon sesame oil
2 tablespoons caster sugar
2 tablespoons Shaoxing rice wine
1 tablespoon *gochugaru* (Korean red chilli powder)
3 dried chillies, halved
250ml (9fl oz) regular soy sauce
800ml (1½ pints) water

3 tablespoons rice wine vinegar
1 spring onion, trimmed and finely chopped

TO SERVE
cooked short-grain rice (see page 26)
Maneul Jangajji (see page 87)

1_ Preheat the oven to 160°C (325°F), Gas Mark 4.

2_ Place the oxtail pieces in a large bowl. Add the flour, salt and pepper and mix together with your hands, ensuring each oxtail piece is thoroughly coated.

3_ Heat the vegetable oil in a heavy-based casserole dish over a high heat. Add the oxtail pieces and cook for 5–6 minutes, turning every couple of minutes, until nicely browned on all sides (you may need to do this in batches to avoid overcrowding the dish). Remove the oxtail from the dish and set aside.

4_ Add the onions and carrots to the casserole dish, lower the temperature to medium and cook, stirring, for 3–4 minutes, until the onions turn translucent and the carrots begin to soften. Return the oxtail to the casserole dish along with all the remaining ingredients except for the rice wine vinegar and spring onion. Stir together well.

5_ Cover the casserole dish with a lid and transfer to the oven. Cook for 4 hours, skimming away any excess fat that floats to the surface every 30 minutes or so, until the meat is tender and slips easily off the bone when pressed gently with a fork. If the meat is still quite firm at this point, return it to the oven for a further 30 minutes until soft.

6_ Once the oxtail is tender, remove the meat and vegetables from the cooking liquid with a slotted spoon and set to one side. Put the casserole dish back on the hob over a high heat and simmer for about 10 minutes until the liquid has reduced by a third and is thick and glossy. Return the oxtail and vegetables to the pan along with the rice wine vinegar and the spring onions and stir together well. Serve with rice and *maneul jangajji* (see page 87).

Mae-Un Jjim Dak SOY-BRAISED CHICKEN

This braised chicken dish is particularly famous in the Korean city of Andong, where there is even a street with a row of restaurants dedicated to serving it. The version they serve there has a distinctly spicy kick, but if you fancy something a little milder and sweeter-tasting, simply take out the chillies.

SERVES
6-8

100g (3½oz) *dangmyeon* sweet potato noodles (see page 162)
6 whole garlic cloves
3 spring onions, trimmed and cut into thirds
1kg (2lb 4oz) bone-in, skin-on chicken thighs or drumsticks

1.5 litres (2½ pints) water, plus extra if needed
5 dried chillies, roughly chopped
5 long red chillies, trimmed and sliced
2 carrots, cut into bite-sized chunks
2 floury potatoes, peeled and cut into bite-sized chunks

SAUCE
150ml (¼ pint) regular soy sauce
2 tablespoons light soy sauce
3 tablespoons caster sugar
pinch of pepper
1½ teaspoons sesame oil

1_ Put the sweet potato noodles in a bowl, cover with boiling water and leave to soak for 15 minutes until soft. Drain and rinse in cold water. Set aside.

2_ For the sauce, combine all the ingredients together in a small bowl.

3_ Put the garlic, spring onions, chillies and chicken pieces in a large heavy-based saucepan or stockpot. Pour over the measurement water (the chicken should be just covered, if not add a little more water) and

bring to the boil. Cook for 15 minutes, keeping the water at a vigorous boil, then ladle out and discard approximately 250ml (9fl oz) of the liquid from the pot. Stir in the sauce, reduce the heat to a simmer and cook for 10 minutes, then add the carrots and potatoes and cook for a further 10 minutes, until the vegetables are tender and cooked through.

4_ Stir the sweet potato noodles through the stew, then ladle it into a large serving dish. Serve in the middle of the table so that everyone can help themselves.

Dak Bokkeum Tang SPICY BRAISED CHICKEN

I first introduced *dak bokkeum tang* (sometimes known as *dak dori tang*) to Gareth as a Korean chicken curry. I guess it is sort of the Korean equivalent, as it has plenty of flavour, lots of spice and a lovely rich sauce. The chicken here should be tender, and the potatoes just a minute or so from falling apart. The potatoes are my favourite part of this dish — they soak up all the delicious flavours from the sauce so well that you'll be fishing them out before anyone else gets a look in.

SERVES
6-8

1kg (2lb 4oz) bone-in, skin-on chicken thighs and legs
2 onions, finely sliced
2 potatoes, cut into 5-cm (2-inch) chunks
750ml (1¼ pints) water

1 carrot, roughly chopped
1 pepper, cored, deseeded and roughly chopped

SAUCE
3 tablespoons *gochujang* (Korean red chilli paste)

4 garlic cloves, minced
3 tablespoons *gochugaru* (Korean red chilli powder)
2 tablespoons regular soy sauce
3 tablespoons caster sugar

1_ Mix together all the sauce ingredients in a small bowl, then add to a large heavy-based saucepan or stockpot with the chicken, onion and potatoes. Pour over the measurement water, bring to a simmer and leave to cook uncovered, stirring occasionally, for 30 minutes.

2_ Stir in the carrot and pepper and simmer gently for a further 30 minutes, until the potatoes are on the point of collapsing and the chicken is tender and almost falling off the bone. Serve with rice.

MAE-UN JJIM DAK

Haemul Bol Jjim SPICY SEAFOOD STEW

My cousin Ji Hyun stayed with us in the UK for a few months one summer so that he could study English and, while he loved it here, the thing he really craved from home was this spicy cod stew. I don't think I'd even tried it back then, but I remember him speaking longingly about it. Having had it since, I can confirm that there really is nothing like it – the seafood gives the delicious spicy sauce loads of flavour, the cod just flakes apart, and the bean sprouts are soft and slippery. If you're a seafood lover, you'll love this.

SERVES
4-6

300g (10½oz) mussels
400g (14oz) bean sprouts
250ml (9fl oz) *Myeulchi Gookmul* (see page 22)
200g (7oz) large raw whole prawns
450g (1lb) cod fillet, deboned and cut into 5-cm (2-inch) squares

50g (1¾oz) chives
cooked short-grain rice (see page 20), to serve

SAUCE
3 tablespoons *gochujang* (Korean red chilli paste)
4 tablespoons *gochugaru* (Korean red chilli powder)

2 tablespoons mirin
8 garlic cloves, finely sliced
1 tablespoon regular soy sauce
1 spring onion, trimmed and finely chopped
1 tablespoon sweet rice flour or corn flour

1_ Sort through the mussels, tapping any that are open lightly on a surface to see if they close shut. Discard the ones that remain open, or any that are damaged. Pull off the beards and scrape any barnacles off using the back of a knife, then rinse.

2_ Bring a saucepan of water to the boil, drop in the bean sprouts and cook for 3–4 minutes until just tender. Drain and rinse under cold running water to cool. Set aside.

3_ Pour the stock into a large heavy-based saucepan and bring to the boil. Reduce the heat to a simmer, add the mussels and prawns and simmer for 3 minutes. Add the cod, cover the pan with a lid and simmer for a further 3–4 minutes until everything is cooked through and the mussels have opened (discard any that remain closed). Remove the pan from the heat and drain away most of the stock, reserving 150ml (¼ pint) in the pan.

4_ Mix the sauce ingredients together in a bowl. Set aside.

5_ Return the pan to a medium-high heat, add the bean sprouts, chives and sauce and gently stir together, being careful not to break up the cod. Simmer for 3–4 minutes, until the chives have wilted and everything is heated through.

6_ Ladle the stew into a large sharing dish and serve in the middle of the table with lots of rice to mop up the spicy sauce.

Mae-Un-Tang FISH MARKET FISH STEW

This dish tastes like Korea to me, its deep-sea flavours conjuring up memories of time spent there in restaurants by the beach. If you order sushi (or *hwe* in Korean) in Korea, this dish is usually served at the end of the meal. The *ajummas* take all the remaining sushi from your table and boil it up along with the chilli paste and any heads and bones from the fish. It's a fantastic way of making sure that nothing is wasted, though it does mean that you're often left with a soup that is full of bones and not a lot of fish! In this version there's plenty of fish to go around.

SERVES
6-8

2.25 litres (4 pints) *Myeulchi Gookmul* (see page 22)
600g (1lb 5oz) mooli, halved lengthways and cut into 5-cm (¼-in) slices
1–2 whole red snapper(s), about 750g (1lb 10oz) in total, descaled, cleaned and cut into 5-cm (2-inch) thick steaks (ask your fishmonger to do this for you)

3 spring onions, trimmed and roughly chopped
1 long red chilli, trimmed and roughly chopped
1 courgette, roughly chopped

PASTE
½ tablespoon *gochujang* (Korean red chilli paste)
½ tablespoon *doenjang* (Korean soybean paste)

3 tablespoons *gochugaru* (Korean red chilli powder)
6 garlic cloves, minced
3 tablespoons light soy sauce
1½ tablespoons fish sauce
pinch of pepper

1_ For the paste, mix together all the ingredients in a bowl. Set aside.

2_ Pour the stock into a large heavy-based saucepan or stockpot and bring to a boil. Add the mooli, reduce to a simmer and cook over a gentle heat for 7–8 minutes, until the mooli begins to soften.

3_ Stir the paste through the broth, add the fish, spring onions, chilli and courgette and simmer for a further 6–7 minutes, until the courgette has softened and the fish is cooked through. Transfer the still-bubbling pan to a heatproof stand in the middle of the table for everyone to help themselves.

Sam Gye Tang CHICKEN AND GINGSENG SOUP

Sam gye tang will always be one of Gareth's most memorable meals from our first trip to Korea together. We went hiking up one of the many mountains in Seoul with my family one weekend and, after a couple of hours, we were feeling pretty tired and ready to rest. As if by magic, we came across a clearing with a stream running directly in front of us. Across the stream, there were two restaurants. An *ajumma* came out of each, beckoning us over for lunch, so we crossed the bridge and settled on the least pushy of the two for an amazing meal of *dotori muk* (acorn jelly), *pajeon* (spring onion pancake) and *sam gye tang*. I'm not sure if perhaps we were really hungry from our trek, or whether it was the fresh mountain air or the fact that the food was simply delicious, but *sam gye tang* quickly became one of Gareth's favourite dishes.

Traditionally, this soup is a summer dish that's eaten on the hottest days of the year (*Sambok*). The idea is that the ginseng causes the temperature of the body to rise, making you sweat and therefore cooling you down. For me though it is warming and comforting, making it perfect for a chilly winter's night.

SERVES 4

125g (4½oz) short-grain rice
1 whole chicken, about 1.5kg (3lb 5oz)
10 whole garlic cloves
80g (3oz) ginseng root, whole
1-cm (½ inch) piece of fresh root ginger, peeled and sliced

6 *jujube* (dried red dates)
3 litres (5¼ pints) water, plus extra if needed

TO GARNISH
2 spring onions, trimmed and finely sliced

TO SERVE
salt
finely ground white pepper

1_ Put the rice in a small bowl, cover with water and leave for 30 minutes to soak. Drain.

2_ If the chicken is trussed, remove any string and open out the legs. Stuff the cavity with the rice and 5 of the garlic cloves, then close up the cavity, folding any loose skin over the opening. Seal with a couple of toothpicks, skewering the skin shut.

3_ Place the chicken in a large, heavy-based saucepan or stockpot and add the gingseng, ginger, *jujube* and the remaining garlic. Pour over the measurement water until the chicken is just covered (adding more if necessary), cover with a lid and bring to the boil. Boil vigorously for 30 minutes, then reduce the heat to a simmer and cook for a further 40 minutes until the chicken is cooked through.

4_ Garnish with the spring onions and serve in the middle of the table with salt and freshly ground white pepper so that everyone can help themselves and season the chicken to their own taste.

TIP: This is often served made from small poussins as individual portions, but we like to eat it as a sharing dish (like the one we had in the mountains). Give each person an empty bowl along with sides of salt and pepper, so that they can take their favourite bits of the chicken, scoop out all the sticky rice from the inside and season to their own taste.

Godeungeo Jorim MACKEREL STEW

This was another one of those dinners that we would have a lot when we were growing up. Mum would whip it together really quickly without having to go to the shops as she'd use tinned mackerel, which we almost always had in our cupboards at home. I like this dish with either fresh or tinned mackerel, but the broth from the fresh mackerel always tastes a little livelier and the mackerel itself goes silky soft. The mooli is my favourite part of this stew, though, as it takes on all the flavours of the sauce – I love to mash it up with my rice with a little bit of the mackerel and a few tablespoons of the liquid... a bit uncouth, maybe, but it must be something I've picked up as my eldest uncle loves to do the same.

SERVES
6

2 mackerel, approximately 500g (1lb 2oz) in total
250g (9oz) mooli, halved lengthways and cut into 1-cm
  (½-inch) thick slices
½ onion, finely sliced
2 long red chillies, roughly chopped

SAUCE
3 tablespoons *gochugaru* (Korean red chilli powder)
5 tablespoons regular soy sauce
2 garlic cloves, finely sliced
250ml (9fl oz) water

1_ Cut along the belly of the mackerel with a sharp knife or scissors, remove the guts and wash the cavities clean. Remove the heads and fins and cut the mackerel into 3-cm (1¼-inch) chunks, leaving the bones in.

2_ For the sauce, mix together the ingredients in a bowl. Set aside.

3_ Arrange the mooli slices on the bottom of a heavy-based saucepan. Add the onion, chilli and mackerel pieces and pour over the sauce. Bring to a simmer, then cover and cook for 30 minutes until the mooli is soft and the mackerel is cooked through.

Miyuk Guk BIRTHDAY SEAWEED SOUP

Although it can be enjoyed anytime, *miyuk guk* is traditionally eaten as a celebratory birthday dish in Korea. In fact, it's one of the first dishes that new mothers eat after having a baby, as it's full of restorative nutrients. On the other hand, if you're sitting any exams this is one to be avoided, as Koreans say that the seaweed is so slippery that you could fail as you might 'slip up' (we're not pulling your leg). My mum loves this dish and its simplicity, whereas I like to add a tablespoon of *gochugaru* at the end for a bit of heat. This is slightly unusual – my cousin and I are the only people I know who eat it this way – but I swear it really lifts the soup. If you want to stick with tradition, leave it out.

SERVES
4

20g (¾oz) dried *miyuk* (wakame) seaweed
150g (5½oz) diced stewing beefsteak
2 tablespoons light soy sauce
pinch of pepper

2 garlic cloves, minced
2 tablespoons sesame oil
1 litre (1¾ pints) water

TO SERVE
gochugaru (Korean red chilli powder), to taste

1_ Put the seaweed in a small bowl, cover with cold water and leave for 10–15 minutes until soft and slippery. Drain and set aside.

2_ Meanwhile, put the beef in a large bowl with the soy sauce, pepper and garlic. Mix all the ingredients together and set aside to marinate for 15 minutes.

3_ Once ready to cook, heat the sesame oil in a large saucepan or stockpot over a medium heat. Add the beef to the pan and fry for 2–3 minutes, stirring, until browned on all sides. Add the seaweed and fry for a further 2 minutes, stirring continuously to prevent the seaweed from sticking to the edges of the pan, then pour over the measurement water and bring to the boil. Reduce the heat and simmer for 30 minutes. Serve with a bowl of chilli powder to add to taste.

Jo-Gae Guk CLEAR CLAM SOUP

The best way to describe this soup is that it tastes just like the sea. It's light and fresh, so it's the perfect accompaniment to spicier, heavier dishes such as *Jeyuk Bokkeum* (see page 108) or *Ojingeo Bokkeum* (see page 129). This is probably one of the most stripped-back Korean dishes there is, with all the ingredients acting to just very gently enhance the natural flavours of the clams.

SERVES
4

450g (1lb) clams
2 tablespoons salt
3 dried *dashima* (kombu) kelp rectangles, about 5cm
   (2 inches) x 3cm (1¼ inches)

3 large dried anchovies
1 litre (1¾ pints) boiling water
30g (1oz) mooli, finely sliced
1 red chilli, trimmed, deseeded and finely sliced
1 spring onion, trimmed and finely sliced

1_ Sort through the clam shells, discarding any that are broken or don't close when tapped gently. Put the remaining clams in a large bowl with the salt and cover with cold water. Cover with aluminium foil, transfer to the refrigerator and leave to soak for 2 hours, then drain and rinse the clams thoroughly under cold running water. Set aside.

2_ Place the dried kelp and anchovies in a large bowl with the measurement water and leave to soak for 10 minutes, then transfer to a large saucepan along with the soaking liquid. Add the mooli, chilli, spring onion, season with salt and bring to the boil.

3_ Once boiling, remove the kelp and anchovies and discard. Add the clams and simmer for 2–3 minutes, skimming off any scum that forms on the surface with a spoon. The clams should now all be open; discard any that are still closed and serve immediately.

Dak Yukgaejang SPICY CHICKEN AND LEEK SOUP

Although this spicy soup is typically made with shredded beef, it never has been in our house. Instead it is always made with chicken or turkey, or more accurately, the leftover bits of chicken and turkey from a Sunday roast or a Christmas dinner. Yet while it may be my mum's equivalent of a Boxing Day turkey curry, it's so much more than just a leftovers dish – in fact, it's actually one of my dad's favourite Korean dishes. The soup is spicy and rich and I particularly love the leeks, which turn silken and slippery soft during cooking. Serve it simply with a side of white rice – and *kimchi*, of course.

SERVES 2

1 tablespoon vegetable oil
150g (5½oz) cooked chicken, shredded
¼ leek, trimmed, cleaned and cut into 5-cm (2-inch) chunks
1 litre (1¾ pints) *Dak Yuksu* (see page 23)

PASTE
1 teaspoon sesame oil
3 tablespoons *gochugaru* (Korean red chilli powder)
6 garlic cloves, minced
1 tablespoon regular soy sauce

TO SERVE
cooked short-grain rice (see page 26)
Baechu Kimchi (see page 32)

1_ For the paste, mix together the ingredients in a small bowl.

2_ Heat the vegetable oil in a large saucepan or stockpot over a medium heat. Add the seasoning paste and fry for 2 minutes, making sure to keep stirring as it catches easily, until fragrant. Add the chicken to the pan, stirring to ensure it is thoroughly coated in the paste, and cook for a further 2 minutes.

3_ Add the leek and pour over the *dak yuksu*. Bring to a simmer and cook for 15 minutes, until the leeks are soft and silky. Serve with rice and *kimchi*.

Gamjatang HANGOVER STEW

Every country has a range of their own special hangover cures, and this is one of Korea's most popular — a hearty, meaty, spicy stew (almost) guaranteed to clear your head after a heavy night. While *gamjatang* translates as 'potato stew', this dish doesn't actually always have potatoes in it, the *gamja* (which ordinarily means 'potato') referring instead to the knobbly pork spine that is traditionally used to make it. Here we've replaced this with the much easier to find pork ribs.

SERVES 6

200g (7oz) new potatoes, halved
1kg (2lb 4oz) pork ribs
1 onion, roughly chopped
2 spring onions, trimmed and roughly chopped
5 whole garlic cloves
2-cm (1-inch) piece of fresh root ginger, peeled and very finely chopped
2.5 litres (4½ pints) water
200g (7oz) *Baechu Kimchi* (see page 32), cut into thin strips and rinsed

50g (1¾oz) chives
125g (4½oz) enoki mushrooms, trimmed

SAUCE
2 tablespoons *gochugaru* (Korean red chilli powder)
12 garlic cloves, finely sliced
2-cm (1-inch) piece of fresh root ginger, peeled and very finely chopped
1 tablespoon light soy sauce
1 tablespoon fish sauce

3 tablespoons mirin
1 tablespoon *gochujang* (Korean red chilli paste)
3 tablespoons *doenjang* (Korean soybean paste)
3 tablespoons perilla seed powder (optional)

TO SERVE
cooked short-grain rice (see page 26)
Baechu Kimchi (see page 32)

1_ For the sauce, mix together the ingredients in a small bowl. Set aside.

2_ Bring a saucepan of water to the boil, add the potatoes and cook for 15 minutes, or until just tender. Drain and rinse under cold running water to cool. Set aside.

3_ Place the ribs in a large saucepan or stockpot with the onion, spring onion, garlic and ginger. Cover with the measurement water, bring to the boil and cook, uncovered, for 1 hour. Stir through the *kimchi* and sauce, reduce the heat to a simmer and cook gently for 15 minutes, then add the potatoes, chives and mushrooms and simmer for a further 2–3 minutes until the potatoes have heated through and the chives have wilted.

4_ Ladle into bowls and serve with rice and *kimchi*.

TIP: Perilla seed powder is made from a herb of the mint family and gives this dish its unique flavour and a slightly numbing, tingly heat. It can be found in Korean supermarkets, but if you can't get hold of it, use a couple of teaspoons of finely ground black pepper instead.

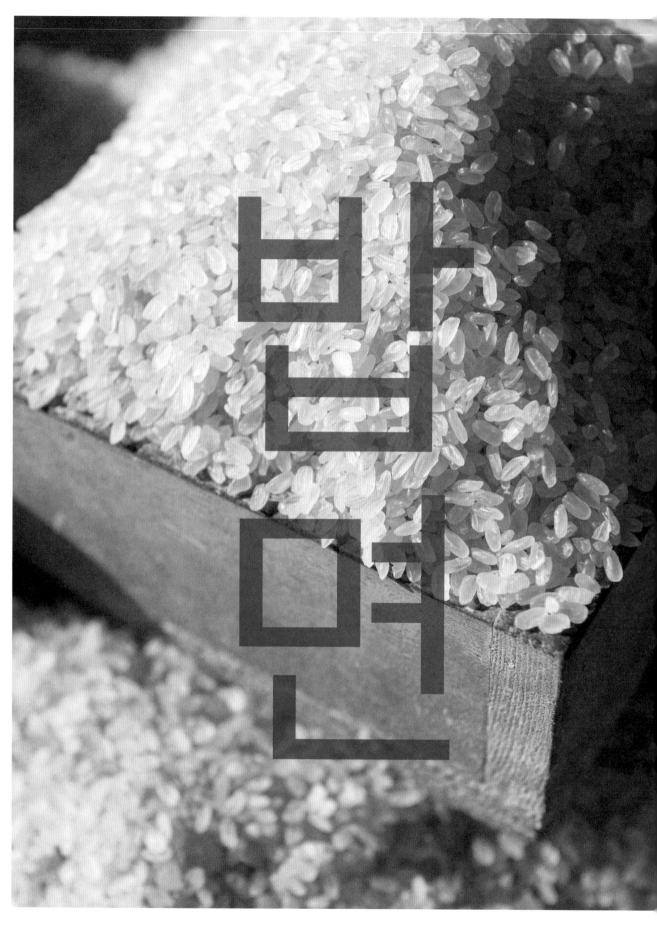

07

Rice & Noodles

If you talk about a

TIGER

IT WILL COME

RICE

Rice is a key part of a Korean diet, so much so that the Korean word for rice, *bap* is the same as the word for food.

Unless noodles are served, short-grain, white (sushi) rice is eaten at every meal and most Koreans will feel like they haven't eaten a complete meal unless they've had a bowl. In fact, even when we go out for Korean BBQ and have had our fill of meat, my family still often orders a few bowls of rice to eat with a *jjigae* to finish the meal.

Korean rice can be eaten plain, mixed with vegetables and *gochujang* to create *bibimbap* or fried to make *bokkeumbap*. In Korea, it's even used as a vehicle for different fillings like a sandwich in the form of *Kimbap*. It can also be turned into the following:

Juk

Rice is often simmered with plenty of water to create a porridge known as *juk*. This is usually eaten when you're feeling unwell — or by the elderly — as it's easy to eat and digest.

Rice Flour and Rice Cakes

Rice can be ground to make a flour (such as sweet rice flour), which can then be used to make Korean rice cakes called *tteok*. Rice flour is also an important ingredient in fermenting *kimchi* and making batters.

Nurungji

When boiling rice, it can often scorch at the bottom of the pan creating a thin layer of crispy rice known as *nurungji*. Nurungji can be eaten as a crispy snack (sometimes sprinkled with a little sugar), or water can be poured into the pan and re-boiled to create *sungnyung*, which is sometimes eaten after a meal to aid digestion.

Alcohol

Korea's biggest-selling spirit *soju* was traditionally made from rice (though it's now often made from a combination of grains and starches). *Soju* is a clear spirit, around 20% ABV and has a slightly sweet, clean flavour that particularly complements spicy or salty foods. Another popular alcohol in Korea is called *makgeolli* which is a rice beer. This creamy drink is made from uncooked rice and a fermentation starter called *nuruk*.

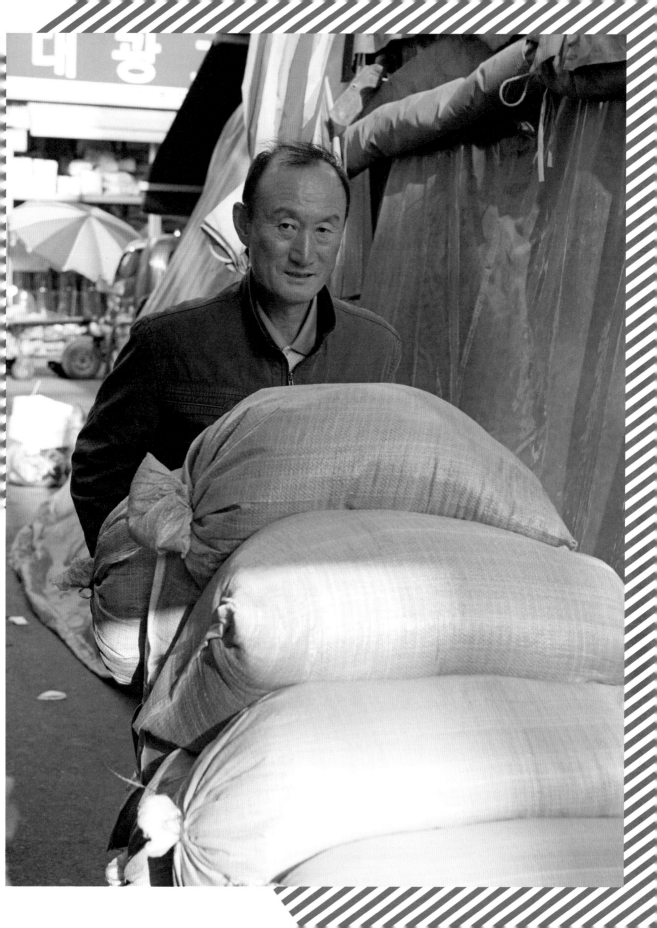

NOODLES

I eat rice almost every day, so I think I'd find it impossible to live without it. It's my comfort food and, particularly when I'm feeling ill, all I want is a bowl of rice and kimchi. My mum however could probably give it up so long as she had noodles in her life. Noodles are my mum's favourite thing to eat, and though she has quite a small appetite the rest of the time, sit her in front of a bowl of noodles and she'll be able to eat them faster than anyone else. There are so many different types of noodles in Korea, so if my mum did give up rice, she'd have plenty of choice. Those we've mentioned in this book include:

Somyun

Somyun are thin vermicelli noodles made from flour. They're quite starchy, so need to be cooked separately and then rinsed and drained before adding them to any soups. *Somyun* noodles can be eaten either hot, like in *Janchi Guksu*, a clear soup traditionally eaten at celebrations, or cold in chilled noodle salads like *Bibim Guksu* (see page 175).

Naengmyeon

Naengmyeon are springy buckwheat noodles that originate from the northern parts of Korea. These noodles are similar to Japanese soba noodles, but they contain sweet potato starch which give them a bouncier, chewier texture. The noodles are slippery (not starchy) and are always enjoyed cold, whether with a spicy sauce or added to a chilled broth like *Mul Naengmyeon* (see page 176).

Dangmyeon

Dangmyeon are also sometimes known as cellophane or glass noodles as they go glossy and transparent when cooked. These noodles are made from sweet potato starch and are usually sold dried in big packets, so they need to be rehydrated in plenty of water before cooking. *Dangmyeon* are the key ingredient in *Japchae* (see page 168) but they're also used in other recipes too, often cut into small pieces to add a little bit of chewy texture, as in the filling for *Gogi Mandu* (see page 53).

Kalguksu

Kalguksu translates as 'knife noodles', as these noodles are traditionally rolled out in large sheets and then cut by hand with a sharp knife. These noodles can also be bought dried, but the texture is very different, so it's best to make your own at home (see page 173). *Kalguksu* are chewy, starchy and very filling.

Ramyun

Ramyun refers to Korean instant noodles, and as they're so popular in Korea, they have to be included here! *Ramyun* are usually wheat noodles that have been pre-fried and come in a large packet, along with some dried vegetables and a seasoning sachet, which creates (an often spicy) noodle broth. The noodles are usually quite springy in texture and are a quick, cheap and convenient option for many Koreans.

A note on noodles: Long noodles are said to symbolize a long life, so for this reason, a lot of people (including my uncle) say that you shouldn't cut them, the idea being that you wouldn't want to cut your life short.

Kimchi Bokkeumbap *KIMCHI* FRIED RICE

Out of all the recipes in this book, this is probably the one that we eat the most often – it's the perfect midweek dinner, as it's really quick and easy to cook. We usually have all the ingredients in our refrigerator and it's a great way to use up leftover rice, as fresh rice here will just make everything a bit mushy. The egg is a must on top – I like mine just-cooked and really runny, so that the yolk mixes into the rice and becomes the sauce. Perfect.

SERVES
2

1 tablespoon vegetable oil, plus extra for frying
100g (3½oz) pork belly, finely chopped
150g (5½oz) *Baechu Kimchi* (see page 32)
1 tablespoon sesame oil
400g (14oz) cooked short-grain rice (see page 26)

1 tablespoon sesame seeds
1 tablespoon *Gochugaru* (Korean chilli powder)
2 spring onions, trimmed and finely sliced
2 eggs

1_ In a heavy-based frying pan, heat the vegetable oil over a medium heat.

2_ Add the pork belly pieces to the pan and cook for 2–3 minutes, stirring, until the edges begin to crisp up and the pork is cooked through. Add the *kimchi* and stir-fry for a further 2–3 minutes, then add the sesame oil, rice, sesame seeds and chilli powder and continue to cook, stirring, until the rice is completely heated through. Stir in the spring onions (reserving a little for garnish) and spoon into bowls.

3_ While the rice is still hot, quickly fry the eggs to your liking in a separate pan. Place a fried egg on the top of each rice bowl and garnish with the reserved spring onions.

Dolsot Bibimbap KOREAN MIXED RICE

Bibimbap literally translates as 'mixed rice' (*bibim* = mixed, *bap* = rice), so you can really throw any ingredients together with some rice and you'd have a form of *bibimbap*. My mum usually makes hers with leftover rice, *Miyuk Muchim* and *Kongnamul Muchim* (see pages 60 and 61) mixed together with some *gochujang* and sesame oil for a quick lunch.

This recipe is the fancier version — *dolsot* refers to the hot stone bowl that the rice is served in. It's served sizzling hot with a raw egg in the middle, which you mix in at the end so you have the texture combination of crispy and soft rice, crunchy vegetables and soft, runny egg. If you don't have a stone bowl, then you can still get the crispy bits by flattening the rice into an even layer in a frying pan instead.

SERVES 2

2–3 dried shiitake mushrooms
vegetable oil
½ carrot, cut into matchsticks
½ courgette, cut into matchsticks
100g (3½oz) *Sigeumchi Muchim* (see page 60)

100g (3½oz) *Kongnamul Muchim* (see page 60)
500g (1lb 2oz) cooked short-grain rice (see page 26)
1 tablespoon sesame oil
1 egg
salt

SAUCE
2 tablespoons *gochujang* (Korean red chilli paste)
1 tablespoon sesame seeds
2 tablespoons sesame oil
½ tablespoon caster sugar
2 garlic cloves, minced

1_ Put the shiitake mushrooms in a bowl and cover with boiling water. Leave to soak for 10 minutes, then strain and slice into thin strips.

2_ Mix all the sauce ingredients together in a small bowl. Set aside.

3_ Heat a splash of oil in a heavy-based pan frying pan over a medium heat. Add the carrot to the pan, season with salt and cook, stirring, for 2–3 minutes until the carrot has softened slightly. Set the carrot aside and repeat with the courgette.

4_ To assemble the dish, heat a Korean *dolsot* stone bowl or a heavy-based frying pan over a high heat for 3–4 minutes until really hot. Brush the inside of the bowl or pan with the sesame oil, then add the rice, pressing it down onto the bottom and up the sides so as much of the surface is covered as possible (this will make sure you get lots of crispy bits).

5_ Once the rice starts to sizzle, start arranging the vegetables in neat piles around the edges, leaving it over a high heat and allowing it to cook for a further 2 minutes to ensure the rice is nice and crispy. Crack the egg in the centre of the *dolsot* or pan, and carefully remove it from the heat. Serve piping hot with the sauce separately, so that you can make it as spicy as you like.

TIP: If you want to make this meaty, add around 50g (1¾oz) of *Yukhoe* (see page 100) to each bowl along with the vegetables. The heat of the hot stone bowl will quickly sear the beef once it's stirred through, so it'll be nicely browned on the outside but still pink in the middle.

Japchae STIR-FRIED 'ROYAL' NOODLES

Along with *bulgogi* and *kimchi*, this is probably one of Korea's most popular and well-known dishes. Historically, these stir-fried sweet potato noodles were enjoyed exclusively by royalty, but now they can be found on any Korean table, particularly when friends and family gather together in celebration. In fact, it's my mum's go-to party-platter dish as it's easy to whip up and can be enjoyed both hot and cold.

SERVES 4 AS A STARTER

SERVES 2 AS A MAIN

4 dried shiitake mushrooms
100g (3½oz) beef frying steak, cut into 5-mm (¼-inch) slices
150g (5½oz) *dangmyeon* sweet potato noodles
3 tablespoons vegetable oil
½ carrot, cut into matchsticks
1 red pepper, cored, deseeded and thinly sliced
2 spring onions, trimmed and cut into 5-cm (2-inch) lengths

100g (3½oz) *Sigeumchi Muchim* (see page 60)

MARINADE
1 tablespoon regular soy sauce
2 garlic cloves, minced
2 teaspoons caster sugar
pinch of pepper

SAUCE
1 tablespoon sesame oil
4 tablespoons regular soy sauce
2 teaspoons caster sugar
2 tablespoons roasted sesame seeds, plus extra to garnish
1 garlic clove, minced
pinch of pepper

1_ Put the shiitake mushrooms in a bowl and cover with boiling water. Leave to soak for 10 minutes, then strain and slice into thin strips.

2_ Meanwhile, mix the marinade ingredients together in a bowl. Add the beef slices and mix well to ensure everything is evenly coated, then leave to marinate for 10 minutes.

3_ Combine the sauce ingredients in another bowl and set aside.

4_ Cook the noodles in boiling water as per the packet instructions, then drain well and rinse under cold water.

5_ Heat 1 tablespoon of vegetable oil in a large frying pan over a medium heat. Add the marinated beef slices and fry for 1–2 minutes until browned, then remove from the pan and set aside.

6_ Add the carrot to the pan and fry for 2 minutes until softened, then add the pepper and spring onions and fry for a further 2 minutes. Remove the vegetables from the pan and set aside, keeping the pan over the heat.

7_ Pour the remaining 2 tablespoons of vegetable oil into the pan, then add the noodles and cook, stirring, for 2 minutes until the noodles are heated through. Add the sauce and all the other ingredients and stir-fry for a further 2 minutes, making sure everything is mixed together and is evenly coated with the sauce.

8_ Divide between bowls, garnish with a few extra sesame seeds and serve immediately.

KNIFE-CUT NOODLES STEP-BY-STEP

1_ Using a rolling pin, roll the dough out into a large rectangular shape, dusting with plenty of flour as you go, until it is about 3mm (¹/₈ inch) thick (be warned, you'll need a large space!).

2_ Run a knife along the outside of the rectangle to straighten the edges and remove any excess dough – this will help you to get even noodles.

3_ Starting from one of the narrow ends of the rectangle, fold over 10cm (4 inches) of the dough. Dust with flour.

4_ Fold and dust with flour again, then repeat until you have reached the other end and are left with a block of dough with layers of folds.

5_ Using a sharp knife, cut the dough block widthways into 5-mm (¼-inch) strips.

6_ Unfold the noodles and dust them with flour. Cover with cling film and set aside until needed. The dough can be made a day ahead but the noodles are best eaten on the day they are rolled and cut.

Kalguksu KNIFE-CUT NOODLES

There's a whole line of stalls in Namdaemun market in Seoul called '*Kalguksu* Alley', where all the *ajummas* are hidden by clouds of steam, huddled over big pans of bubbling stock, each making *kalguksu* to their own special recipe. My favourite place to enjoy this noodle broth, though, is a standalone hut in the middle of the hustle and bustle of the main market as the *ajummas* there are amazingly skilled, deftly making noodles at amazing speed due to their years of experience. There are faded menus on the walls displaying a selection of different dishes, but everyone who visits is there to eat the noodles. Each table has a little earthenware pot of very fermented *kimchi* that you help yourself to – the tangy chilli heat cuts through the starchy, chewy noodles and is the perfect match.

SERVES
4

2 litres (3½ pints) *Dak Yuksu* (see page 23)
1 courgette, cut into thin matchsticks
100g (3½oz) cooked chicken meat, shredded

NOODLES
600g (1lb 5oz) plain flour, plus extra for dusting
4 tablespoons sweet rice flour

2 teaspoons salt
300ml (½ pint) water

TO GARNISH
1 dried *gim* (nori) seaweed sheet, finely sliced
2 tablespoons roasted sesame seeds
1 spring onion, trimmed and finely sliced

TO SERVE
Yangnyum Jang (see page 21)
matured *Baechu Kimchi* (see page 32)

1_ To make the noodles, in a large bowl combine the flour, rice flour and salt. Pour over the water a little at a time and stir together with a wooden spoon until the mixture begins to stick together. Using your hands, shape the mixture into a rough ball, then tip it onto a clean, floured surface and knead it for 10 minutes until it is smooth and elastic.

2_ Wrap the dough ball in clingfilm and refrigerate for 20 minutes, then return the dough to the floured work surface and knead for a further 10 minutes, adding a little extra flour as you go to stop the dough from sticking. Roll out and cut the noodles following the step-by-step instructions on the previous page.

3_ Bring the stock to a vigorous boil in a large saucepan and add the courgette and cooked chicken and heat for 2 minutes until the courgette has softened. Add the noodles to the pan and cook for 3 minutes, or until the noodles are cooked through, stirring using a fork or pasta tongs to prevent the noodles from sticking together.

4_ Ladle the noodles into large bowls, scatter over the seaweed, sesame seeds and spring onion to garnish and serve with *yangnyum jang* and strong *baechu kimchi*, so that each person can adjust to taste.

Dangmyeon Bokkeum SPICY STIR-FRIED VEGGIE NOODLES

Strangely enough, this vegetarian- and vegan-friendly dish is actually based on *soondae bokkeum*, a real meat-eater's meal made with a blood sausage called *soondae*, the Korean version of black pudding. This adaptation focuses on the dish's best bit, its spicy sauce, which clings here to the sweet potato noodles, making them deliciously sticky and irresistible to even the most hardcore of carnivores.

SERVES
4

10 dried shiitake mushrooms
150g (5½oz) *dangmyeon* sweet potato noodles
6 tablespoons vegetable oil
1 aubergine, cut into 1-cm (½-inch) cubes
2 garlic cloves, minced
2 bird's eye chillies, trimmed and chopped
pinch of salt
1 onion, thinly sliced
½ red cabbage, thinly sliced

500g (1lb 2oz) chestnut mushrooms, sliced

SAUCE
2 tablespoons *gochugaru* (Korean red chilli powder)
2 tablespoons *gochujang* (Korean red chilli paste)
2 tablespoons regular soy sauce
2 tablespoons sesame oil
2 tablespoons clear runny honey
6 garlic cloves, minced

1 tablespoon *soju* (Korean rice spirit) or mirin
2 tablespoons apple vinegar
2 tablespoons perilla seed powder or 2 teaspoons finely ground black pepper

TO GARNISH
2 spring onions, trimmed and finely chopped
2 tablespoons roasted sesame seeds
1 dried *gim* (nori) seaweed sheet, sliced into thin matchsticks

1_ Put the shiitake mushrooms in a bowl and cover with boiling water. Leave to soak for 10 minutes, then strain, setting aside the soaking water, and slice into thin strips.

2_ Meanwhile, cook the noodles in boiling water as per the packet instructions, then drain well and rinse under cold water. Set aside.

3_ To make the sauce, put all the ingredients together in a bowl and mix together well, stirring in a tablespoon of the mushroom soaking water to loosen the mixture a little.

4_ Heat 3 tablespoons of the vegetable oil in a large frying pan over a medium heat. Add the aubergine and cook, stirring, for 3 minutes until softened, then add the garlic, chillies and salt and cook for a further 2–3 minutes. Tip the aubergine onto a plate and set to one side.

5_ Put the pan back over a medium heat with the remaining 3 tablespoons of vegetable oil. Add the onion, lower the heat and cook gently, stirring occasionally, for 10 minutes, until the onion is softened but not brown.

6_ Add the shiitake mushrooms to the pan along with the cabbage and chestnut mushrooms. Increase the heat to medium and stir-fry for 5–6 minutes, then add the noodles and sauce, tossing or stirring everything together so that the noodles are completely coated and the ingredients are evenly distributed. Continue cooking for 2–3 minutes until the noodles are heated through, stirring to ensure they don't stick to the bottom of the pan.

7_ Garnish with spring onion, sesame seeds and seaweed strips to serve.

Bibim Guksu SUMMER NOODLE SALAD
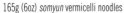

These spicy noodles are a great way to use up any leftover salad or crunchy veg you may have lurking in your refrigerator, so don't feel bound by the carrots and iceberg lettuce we use here. My mum likes to add the (slightly unusual) combination of rocket and watercress to hers to give it a really peppery kick. Serving this with the Korean egg drop soup will help extinguish some of the heat.

SERVES
2

165g (6oz) *somyun* vermicelli noodles
1 green apple, cored and cut into thin strips
¼ iceberg lettuce, shredded
1 carrot, halved and cut into thin strips
1 spring onion, trimmed and finely sliced, plus extra to garnish
3 tablespoons *gochujang* (Korean red chilli paste)
1 tablespoon *gochugaru* (Korean red chilli powder)

2 garlic cloves, minced
1½ tablespoons caster sugar
3½ tablespoons apple vinegar
1 teaspoon roasted sesame seeds
1 teaspoon sesame oil
2 hard-boiled eggs, peeled and sliced, to garnish

GYERAN GUK (KOREAN EGG DROP SOUP)
500ml (18fl oz) *Myeulchi Gookmul* (see page 22)
1 tablespoon light soy sauce
2 spring onions, trimmed and finely chopped
2 eggs, beaten

TO SERVE
English mustard
apple vinegar

1_ Cook the noodles in boiling water according to the packet instructions, then drain well and rinse under cold water.

2_ Squeeze out any excess water from the noodles and put them in a large bowl with all the remaining ingredients except the hard-boiled eggs. Mix everything together well, then divide between bowls.

3_ For the *gyeran guk*, put the stock in a saucepan with the soy sauce and spring onions and bring to the boil. Add the beaten egg to the boiling stock, using a chopstick or a spoon to ensure the ribbons are distributed evenly through the liquid. Allow the egg to cook for 20–30 seconds until lightly cooked, then pour into side bowls.

4_ Garnish the *bibim guksu* with the hard-boiled egg slices and a little extra spring onion. Serve with the soup, along with mustard and vinegar to season to your own taste.

Mul Naengmyeon CHILLED NOODLE SOUP

| Along with *Bibim Guksu* (see page 175) this is one of my favourite things to eat in the summer. Made from buckwheat, these noodles are springy and chewy – a completely different texture to the soft *somyun* vermicelli noodles typically used in Korean soups. I like to add loads of vinegar and mustard to the ice cold broth here, often so much that it makes me suck in my cheeks and gives me a severe case of 'mustard nose'

SERVES
2

250g (9oz) *naengmyeon* buckwheat noodles
10 ice cubes, crushed
½ Asian pear, peeled, cored and thinly sliced
150g (5½oz) beef frying steak, thinly sliced and cooked to your liking
2 hard-boiled eggs, peeled

BROTH
1 litre (1¾ pints) beef stock
3 whole garlic cloves

2-cm (¾-inch) piece of fresh root ginger, whole
1 spring onion, trimmed and roughly chopped
1 tablespoon light soy sauce
2 tablespoons apple vinegar

SAUCE
½ Asian pear, peeled, cored and puréed
1 spring onion, trimmed and finely sliced
1 tablespoon regular soy sauce
1 tablespoon *gochugaru* (Korean red chilli powder)

1 teaspoon caster sugar
1 teaspoon apple vinegar
2 garlic cloves, minced
1-cm (½-inch) piece of fresh root ginger, peeled and very finely chopped
½ teaspoon roasted sesame seeds

TO SERVE
English mustard
apple vinegar

1_ Put all the broth ingredients in a large saucepan and bring to a boil. Reduce the heat and simmer over a medium heat for 10 minutes, then strain the broth through a sieve. Pour the strained broth into a large bowl and leave in the refrigerator for about 30 minutes until cooled.

2_ While the stock is chilling, mix the sauce ingredients together in a small bowl. Set aside.

3_ Cook the noodles in boiling water according to the packet instructions, then drain well and rinse under cold water.

4_ Divide the ice cubes, noodles, pear and steak between two serving bowls, then pour half of the chilled stock over each.

5_ Halve the eggs and arrange on top of the noodles. Spoon over the sauce and serve with English mustard and apple vinegar for adding to the broth as you like.

Ramyun INSTANT NOODLES

Ramyun (or instant noodles) are so loved by Koreans that they consume more of them per head than anyone else in the world. In most corner shops in Korea you'll find a *ramyun* area where you can take your cup of instant noodles, fill it at the hot water station and sit in store on the plastic benches to eat your speedy meal. To Koreans, *ramyun* are more than a quick and easy fast food though – people genuinely love the taste, and most have their own way of customizing them to turn them into a hearty and substantial meal. We've included our favourite ways of eating these noodles here, as well as asking some of our friends how they eat theirs. We also recommend using Korean instant noodles in a hot and spicy flavour – we normally eat the *Shin Ramyun* brand at home, so the recipes below are based on this.

JUDY JOO'S *RAMYUN*
Executive Chef of Jinjuu Restaurant

Throw away your noodle seasoning packet and make your own broth by mixing 2 tablespoons *gochujang* (Korean red chilli paste) and 1 teaspoon *doenjang* (Korean soybean paste) into some chicken stock in a saucepan. Bring to the boil and add your instant noodles along with whatever you have in your refrigerator (for me this is usually some combination of spring onions, Chinese cabbage, seaweed, chopped red chillies, prawns, shredded chicken, tofu or egg), until noodles are cooked.

LIZZIE MABBOTT'S *RAMYUN*
Author of *Chinatown Kitchen*

Cook your instant noodles as per the packet instructions along with the seasoning packet. Fry some Spam chunks in a dry, nonstick pan until crisp, then add these to the drained noodles. Top with a soft-boiled egg and finish with a drizzle of ginger and spring onion oil and a good shake of *shichimi togarashi* (Japanese spice mix).

JOE MCPHERSON'S *RAMYUN*
Founder of ZenKimchi.com

Boil your instant noodles in water (without the seasoning packet) and drain once cooked. Heat a little vegetable oil in a pan and throw in the drained noodles along with the seasoning from the *ramyun* packet. Crack in an egg, and scramble it in. Toss in some pasta sauce and mix in until just heated through. My brother swears by this!

DA-HAE'S *RAMYUN*

550ml (1 pint) water
2–3 bird's eye chillies, finely sliced
50g (1¾oz) mature *Baechu Kimchi* (see page 32),
    drained and roughly chopped
50g (1¾oz) pork belly, cut into matchsticks

1 x 120g (4½oz) hot and spicy *Shin Ramyun* instant
    noodle packet
1 spring onion, trimmed and finely sliced
1 egg

1_ Bring the measurement water to the boil in a
saucepan along with the chillies, *kimchi* and pork
belly. Add the noodles, noodle seasoning packet and
spring onion and continue to cook for 2 minutes.

2_ Turn off the heat, make a well in the middle of the
noodles with a chopstick or fork and crack in the egg.
Pile the noodles carefully over the egg to cover, then
put the lid on the pan and leave for 2 minutes for the
egg to poach. Serve immediately – the egg whites
should be firm and the yolk perfectly poached.

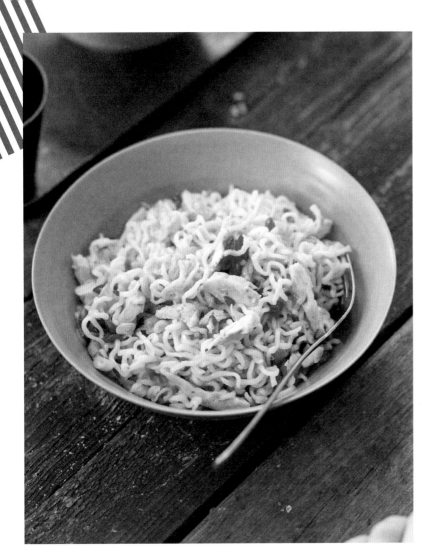

GARETH'S *RAMYUN*

1 x 120g (4½oz) hot and spicy *Shin Ramyun* instant
   noodle packet
1 bird's eye chilli, finely sliced
1 tablespoon vegetable oil

75g (2½oz) cooked chicken meat, shredded
1 processed cheese slice
1 tablespoon grated medium Cheddar cheese
2 spring onions, finely sliced

1_ Put the noodles in a saucepan with the chilli, pour over enough boiling water to cover and cook (without the seasoning packet) for 1–2 minutes, until the noodles are al dente and just cooked. Drain and set aside.

2_ Heat the oil in a frying pan over a medium heat. Add the chicken and fry for 2–3 minutes until heated through. Add the drained noodles along with the seasoning from the noodle packet and fry for a further minute, stirring everything together to make sure the noodles are evenly coated in the seasoning.

3_ Tip the noodles into a large bowl and top with the processed and grated cheeses. Cover with a plate and leave for 2 minutes for the cheese to melt a little, then scatter over the spring onions and serve.

Drinks & Drinking Culture

08

At the end of hardship comes

HAPPINESS

If you've ever been to Korea – or even seen the video for Psy's Hangover – you'll have some idea of what drinking in Korea is like. Drinking is an important part of Korean culture because Koreans see it as an important way of forming bonds and relationships, as it makes people let their guard down. In fact, there's even a saying which translates as, 'one glass isn't enough, three's too little, five's the right number and seven's pushing the limit'. I've heard my uncle say this before and it's a rule I'm pretty sure he sticks to.

The most popular alcohol in Korea is *soju*, which was traditionally made by distilling rice and water. Nowadays, the mass-produced varieties contain a mixture of grains (including wheat, barley and tapioca) along with ethanol, water and sweeteners. It's cheap (and so is an easy way to get drunk) as one bottle of standard 375ml (13fl oz), 19 per cent ABV *soju* normally costs around ₩1200 or about £0.75. *Soju* is a clear spirit, like vodka but it tastes a little sweeter and feels smoother. It's usually served chilled and poured into shot glasses, though there's a real culture of mixing your drinks in Korea, which we'll go into more detail on later. As well as *soju*, other popular drinks include:

Makgeolli

Makgeolli is a fermented drink (some say rice wine, some say rice beer) made with rice using a Korean fermentation starter called nuruk. It's a creamy, cloudy drink that's slightly sweet and a little bit fizzy. It's about six per cent ABV and is usually drunk from metal or wooden bowls. Traditionally favoured by farmers and the elderly (it's often considered to be quite filling), *makgeolli* used to be a pretty unfashionable drink, though that's now changed with the rise of *makgeolli* bars which sell different variations of it, including chestnut, *yuja* (yuzu), berry and sesame.

Beer

Beer or *mekju* as it's called in Korean is very popular. The Korean brands OB, Cass and Hite dominate the market with their light, easy-to-drink beer. People more used to Western-style beers often find Korean beer quite watery and weak, but as it's so light, it's makes a great accompaniment to Korean food, which is often full of strong flavours.

Bekseju

Bekseju or 'one-hundred-year-old wine' refers to how old you might live to be when drinking it due to its apparent health properties. *Bekseju* is made with Korean sweet (glutinous) rice and is flavoured with ginseng and 11 other herbs including ginger, cinnamon and liquorice – all of which combined are said to help you live a long life. A little sweet, the predominant ginseng flavour can taste quite medicinal at first until you get used to it.

Sansachun

Sansachun is another drink known for its medicinal properties, and is said to help calm your nerves. Supposedly, a shot of this a day will keep the doctor away. *Sansachun* is made from the red berries of the *sansa* (hawthorn) and is very sweet and syrupy, so it's best enjoyed before a meal rather than with food.

Bokbunja

Bokbunja is a syrupy wine made with black raspberries that is usually between 15–19 per cent ABV. It's sweet, mild and deep red in colour, and works really well with desserts – I like to pour it all over an Eton mess as the flavour really complements the berries and meringues. It's said to help promote 'male stamina' (like a lot of things which are said to be good for the health in Korea), and so is a popular drink with honeymooners. The best thing about *bokbunja* though has to be its translation, which is 'a force so strong, it could knock a urinal over', illustrating perfectly how easy to drink it is.

Maesilju

Maesilju is made from small green plums called *maesil*. It usually comes in a green bottle with a wide top with a few plums at the bottom. It's sweet and tart as the plums are usually fermented with plenty of sugar, and it's usually drunk from small shot glasses like *soju*, but can also be enjoyed as a dessert wine or in cocktails.

DRINKING RULES

People new to Korean drinking culture are often surprised by how many rules there are. These rules include:

- Drink the drink you're given. It's considered very rude to refuse a drink – even if you're not a big drinker, you'd be expected to at least take the first glass.
- Make sure to pour and receive drinks with both hands, unless you're drinking with friends, or if you're the eldest.
- The first drink should be with everyone all together, so that you can 'cheers' or *gumbae* in Korean.
- The youngest at the table should pour the drink, unless someone older takes it from them.
- Never fill your own glass, particularly if it's a sharing bottle such as *soju*. Always keep an eye on everyone else's glasses to be ready to pour them a drink so that their glass doesn't sit empty – Koreans also believe that you shouldn't top up a glass that is half-filled (you should wait until that person has drained their shot).

HWESHIK

Most companies in Korea will take part in something called *hweshik* which translates as 'company dinner', as it combines the words *hwesa* (company) and *shiksa* (meal). These company meals are held on a regular basis (once or twice a month) and are pretty mandatory if you want to get anywhere in business. *Hweshik* is more than just eating together and is very different to the average company get-together in the UK as it's actually an event that takes place in several rounds called *il cha*, *ee cha*, *sam cha*, *sa cha* (and if you're still standing, *o cha*) – rounds one, two, three, four and five, with each round taking place in a different location.

Il Cha (1)

Hweshiks usually kick off at a Korean BBQ restaurant, with the boss ordering meat (usually *samgyeopsal*, see page 92) for the entire table along with plenty of drink (usually beer and *soju*).

Ee Cha (2)

After the barbecue, the next place is the pub, or *hof* as it's called in Korean. This will include more food called *anju* (usually Korean Fried Chicken, see page 212) and a few bottles of *soju* will be ordered.

Sam Cha (3)

Sam cha is often another *hof* for a change of scenery and plenty more drinks. At this point, there will be a lot more drinking games going on.

Sa Cha (4)

For round four, everyone then moves over to the *noraebang* or karaoke. Karaokes can be found all over Korea and are usually private rooms with a big screen, a fat book of songs to choose from and a few tambourines. It doesn't matter if you don't have the best voice, as the whole thing is more about the bonding experience, but if you want to save face some people (members of my family included) practice four to five songs to make sure they're able to belt them out perfectly when their time comes.

O Cha (5)

If you have the stamina to last until *o cha* (impressive), then it's time to move to a club for more drinks and lots of dancing, often until the sun starts to rise…

MIXING DRINKS

Mixing your drinks is very common in Korea, with 'bomb' type drinks being particularly popular – and not just reserved for university students. Even when President Lee Myung Bak was in office, he'd always drink *soju* bombs when he was drinking in public with other high-ranking officials.

Somek

The most popular *soju* mix is *somek* – a glass of beer mixed with *soju*. You put a glass of *soju* at the bottom of a beer glass, pour beer up to the rim and stick a chopstick in the centre which you then hit hard with the other chopstick to cause bubbles to rise and mix everything together. Another way to mix a *somek* is to line up a row of beers with shots of *soju* balanced in between them to create a *soju* train. The first *soju* shot is then flicked over so that all the *soju* glasses fall into the beer in a domino effect.

Go-jin-gam-rae

Translating as 'no pain, no gain', this drink is a combination of cola, *soju* and beer. Place a shot glass three-quarters full of cola at the bottom of a beer glass followed by an empty shot glass on top which you fill with *soju*. Beer is then poured in the gap next to the glasses until it reached the top, with the idea being to drink this all in one (or 'one shot' as Koreans say) so that you get the fizz of the beer, followed by the *soju* and then ending with the sweetness of cola.

O-Sip-Se-Ju

Bekseju or 'one-hundred-year-old wine' becomes *o-sip-se-ju* or 'fifty-year-old wine' when mixed in equal quantities of *soju*.

So-baek-san-mek

This drink is named after the initials of all the component drinks and is a simple mix of equal parts of *soju*, *bekseju*, *sansachun* and *mekju* (beer). This is often done by the bottle in a big jug.

HANGOVER CURES

Due to having such a big drinking culture, Korea has a *lot* of hangover cures. The most popular include soups such as *Gamjatang* (see page 157), bean sprout soup, *haejangguk* (which literally translates as 'hangover cure soup') and dried pollock soup.

There are also lots of different energy drinks that you can buy at the convenience store (or pharmacy if you're in need of something stronger) in small brown or green bottles which you down in one shot to get rid of a hangover. One of the most popular is called Condition – you drink one before you start drinking any alcohol and then one the next day, and most Koreans will swear that you won't feel a thing, no matter how much you've had to drink the night before.

DRINKING GAMES

Gareth has been introduced to a whole host of different drinking games by my cousins, which include the following:

Flicking the Soju Cap

The common green *soju* bottles have a metal screw-top lid. As you open the bottle, you're often left with a metal thread dangling from the side, which you twist in on itself to create a little stick. Everyone around the table has a turn flicking the stick – the winner is the person who is able to get the stick to fly off and the person before them has to drink a shot.

Baskin Robbins 31

I'm not sure why this is called Baskin Robbins, but basically everyone around the table counts up to three numbers in order. For example: one or one, two or one, two, three. This goes around the group until it gets to 30 – whoever 31 lands on must drink.

Three, Six, Nine

Go around the table and count in order starting from one. Any time a number has a three, six or nine in it, the person has to clap – until the numbers reach double figures (33, 36, 39), in which case you have to clap twice on these numbers. Whoever says the wrong number or claps in the wrong place (or forgets to clap twice) has to drink a shot.

Titanic

Fill a glass with beer and then float an empty shot glass on top. Everyone has a turn pouring a little bit of alcohol into the shot glass and whoever makes it sink has to drink.

Everyone Drinks

Each person takes turns to get everyone else around the table to have a drink by coming up with criteria for those who have to take a shot. For example, 'all the people wearing jeans, drink', or 'all the men over 20, drink'. This game is fast-paced and dangerous as it's so open to stitching someone up.

The Black Knight/Rose

If you've reached a point in your evening where you really can't drink anymore, you can nominate a Black Knight (for men) or Black Rose (for women) as someone to take your drink for you. By doing this though, your ball is very much in the Black Knight or Rose's court as they can think up the terms of repayment (a favour or dare) and then there's always the risk that they might refuse you, in which case you have to drink two shots instead... it's a pretty risky business and only really suggested for desperate times!

Kimchi Bloody Mary

In Korea, eating and drinking with your colleagues (and boss) is an important part of team bonding called *hweshik*. This midweek drinking culture means that hangovers can be a common problem, which explains Korea's many different hangover cures. Here we've taken the traditional Bloody Mary recipe but given it a bit of an extra Korean chilli kick with the *kimchi* and *gochugaru*. We've also decorated this drink with bean sprouts as a cheeky nod to the (many) Korean hangover soups in which they feature.

SERVES
1

1 long red chilli, trimmed, deseeded and finely chopped
ice cubes
35ml (1¼fl oz) vodka
25ml (1fl oz) *soju* (Korean rice/grain spirit)
50ml juice drained from *kimchi*

70ml (2½fl oz) tomato juice
2 teaspoons lime juice
½ teaspoon Worcestershire sauce

TO DECORATE
1 tablespoon *gochugaru* (Korean red chilli powder)
¼ lime
3–4 beansprouts
1 celery stick

1_ Put the chilli at the bottom of a pint glass and squash it with the end of a rolling pin (or muddler if you have one) to release its flavour.

2_ Fill the glass with ice cubes, then add the vodka, *soju*, *kimchi* juice, tomato juice, lime juice and Worcestershire sauce. Pour the cocktail into a second pint glass, then return it to the original glass. Repeat the process 3 times (the aim is to chill the cocktail without melting the ice and diluting the drink).

3_ Spread the *gochugaru* evenly over a small plate. Run the lime quarter along the rim of a highball glass, then dip the rim of the glass in the *gochugaru* to coat. Fill the glass with ice cubes, strain over the cocktail mix and decorate with a few bean sprouts and a celery stick to serve.

Apple and Chilli Smash

When I order something from a menu that says it has chilli in it, I really want to be able to feel that chilli heat. Now, I don't necessarily mean I want my head blown off, but I definitely want to know that there's some chilli in there. That's why I love this drink in which the sour apple contrasts with the chilli's prickly, fruity heat. It'll leave your tongue tingling.

SERVES
1

½ lime, cut into quarters
½ apple, cut into 1-cm (½-inch) cubes
1 red chilli, trimmed, deseeded and roughly chopped
2 teaspoons caster sugar

50ml (2fl oz) apple vodka
crushed ice
50ml (2fl oz) clear lemonade
1 red bird's eye chilli, to decorate

1_ Put the lime, apple, chopped chilli and sugar in a jug. Using the end of a rolling pin (or a cocktail muddler if you have one), squash the ingredients together to let their flavours infuse.

2_ Pour the apple vodka into a highball glass and fill with crushed ice. Tip the smashed lime and apple mix into the glass and stir together well with a cocktail spoon. Pour over the lemonade.

3_ Cut a slit in the middle of the bird's eye chilli and prop on the rim of the glass to decorate and serve.

Grown-up Yakult

Ever since I was little, I've been a bit addicted to Yakult. For me the milky probiotic is a real reminder of Korea (I drank at least three to four bottles a day when I was there) and even now my aunt always has some in her refrigerator ready for me when I visit, as she knows how much I love it. Combining it with *soju* might sound a bit intimidating, but along with the lemonade, this cocktail actually ends up tasting like fizzy sweets. Trust me.

SERVES
1

ice cubes
70ml (2½fl oz) *soju* (Korean rice/grain spirit)
1 Yakult (65ml/2¼fl oz)
70ml (2½fl oz) lemonade

Fill a highball glass with ice cubes. Pour over the *soju*, Yakult and the lemonade to finish. Stir together with a cocktail spoon and serve.

Soju Mule

This cocktail was the most popular drink at our first ever pop-up in Tooting market. It is almost sinfully simple but the sweetness of the *soju* balances brilliantly against the sourness of the lime and the bitterness of the Angostura. This drink is amazing served in a huge jug filled with ice for friends to share on a summer's day.

SERVES
1

ice cubes
1 lime, cut into eighths
10 drops of Angostura bitters

70ml (2½fl oz) *soju* (Korean rice/grain spirit)
80ml (2¾fl oz) ginger beer

1_ Fill a highball glass with ice cubes.

2_ Squeeze the lime segments over the ice, then drop them into the glass. Pour over the Angostura bitters, *soju* and ginger beer. Stir together with a cocktail spoon and serve.

Baesuk Martini

Definitely one for those with a sweet tooth, *Baesuk* is a traditional Korean punch made from steamed pear, cinnamon, honey and *jujube*. Here these flavours combine perfectly with rum to create a lightly spiced martini version of this Korean sweet treat.

SERVES 1

1 x 410g (14oz) tin pears in syrup
1 cinnamon stick
1 tablespoon clear runny honey
ice cubes

15ml (½fl oz) spiced light rum
35ml (1¼fl oz) vodka
1 *jujube* (dried red date), to decorate (optional)

1_ Drain the syrup from the pears into a saucepan and set the pears to one side.

2_ Add the cinnamon stick and honey to the pan and heat gently for 2–3 minutes, stirring, until the honey has dissolved. Remove from the heat and set aside for 5 minutes to allow the flavours to infuse, then remove the cinnamon stick and leave for a further 5 minutes to cool.

3_ Fill a martini glass with ice cubes to chill, then tip the ice out.

4_ Fill a pint glass with ice cubes. Pour over the rum, vodka and 50ml (2fl oz) of the cooled syrup and gently stir the ingredients together with a cocktail spoon.

5_ Place the *jujube* at the bottom of the martini glass and strain over the cocktail mix.

HongCho Collins

HongCho is a flavoured drinking vinegar with added fruit concentrate. In Korea, it's usually enjoyed in the summer, mixed with sparkling water and poured over ice, as a tangy, refreshing drink. This cocktail mixes HongCho with soju – the tang of the drinking vinegar taking away the harsh alcoholic edge of the spirit. Dangerously delicious, it's perhaps a little too easy to drink…

SERVES 1

ice cubes
70ml (2½fl oz) soju (Korean rice/grain spirit)
70ml (2½fl oz) pomegranate HongCho
25ml (1fl oz) lemon juice
35ml (1¼fl oz) bokbunja (Korean berry wine)

25ml (1fl oz) sugar syrup
soda water, to top up

TO DECORATE
slice of lemon
1 tablespoon pomegranate seeds

1_ Fill a highball glass with ice cubes and set aside.

2_ Fill a cocktail shaker with ice cubes. Add the soju, HongCho, lemon juice, bokbunja and sugar syrup and shake vigorously for about 1 minute, or until a frost forms on the side of the shaker.

3_ Strain the cocktail into the highball glass and top up with soda water. Decorate with a slice of lemon and some pomegranate seeds.

TIP: Make up your own sugar syrup by stirring together equal parts of caster sugar and water until the sugar has dissolved.

Anju & Bar Snacks

09

STARTING IS Half the JOB

In Korea it is very difficult to go for a drink without food. The very fact that Korean has a specific word, *anju*, to describe the food that you eat when drinking shows how the two are linked and (outside of westernized districts) Korean hofs or pubs will expect you to order something to eat whenever you order any drinks. This is partly because the alcohol is generally very cheap, but also because drinking is a sociable experience best enjoyed in a group with plenty of food to share. Plus, it's never a bad idea to line your stomach when drinking.

The recipes we've included here are the messy kind of fast-food style *anju* that we love. They're mostly designed for sharing and are perfect with a few shots of *soju* or beer.

READING AN *ANJU* MENU

When you arrive at a *hof* you are usually given a menu which is split into several categories of *anju*:

Chicken

Korean fried chicken is the ultimate *anju* for us. Double-fried, super-crispy, juicy chicken is the perfect accompaniment to an ice-cold beer. It's usually available plain, with either sweet-and-spicy or soy glazes, or with piles of finely chopped garlic on top. The chicken is usually served with two forks per person – so that you can pull the meat apart without getting your fingers too dirty – and with a side of pickled mooli to help cleanse the palate between bites.

Soups and Stews

Soups and stews eaten as *anju* are usually quite spicy or salty as that pairs well with most Korean alcohol, which acts as palate cleanser. Examples include bean sprout soup (some people believe that it prevents a hangover if they eat it while they're drinking), *kimchi jjigae* and *ramyun*.

Deep-fried

Deep-fried *anju* are pretty varied and can include tempuras, chips and even potato smiley faces. Gareth and my dad have ordered 'assorted fried potato' from a *hof* before, thinking that they might receive a plate of chips, but what they were actually given was a mixture of hash browns, French fries, smiley faces and deep-fried balls of mash.

Dried

Dried *anju* are the ones we'd normally go for on days when we're feeling really, really full. Dried *anju* are usually a choice of dried or partially dried squid (accompanied by ketchup and mayo for dipping), dried and sweetened filefish (a type of tropical fish), dried anchovies and/or nuts. These are often served with M&M peanuts.

Fruit

For those wanting a healthier or lighter option, you can always order a platter of fruit, or one of fruit and ham. These platters tend to be quite expensive, usually a similar price to a plate of fried chicken, which is why we never end up ordering them.

Traditional

Other than the soups and stews, traditional *anju* include *dubu kimchi* (steamed tofu with *kimchi* and fried pork), steamed silkworm *pupae* (not a favourite of ours) and *pajeon* (spring onion pancakes).

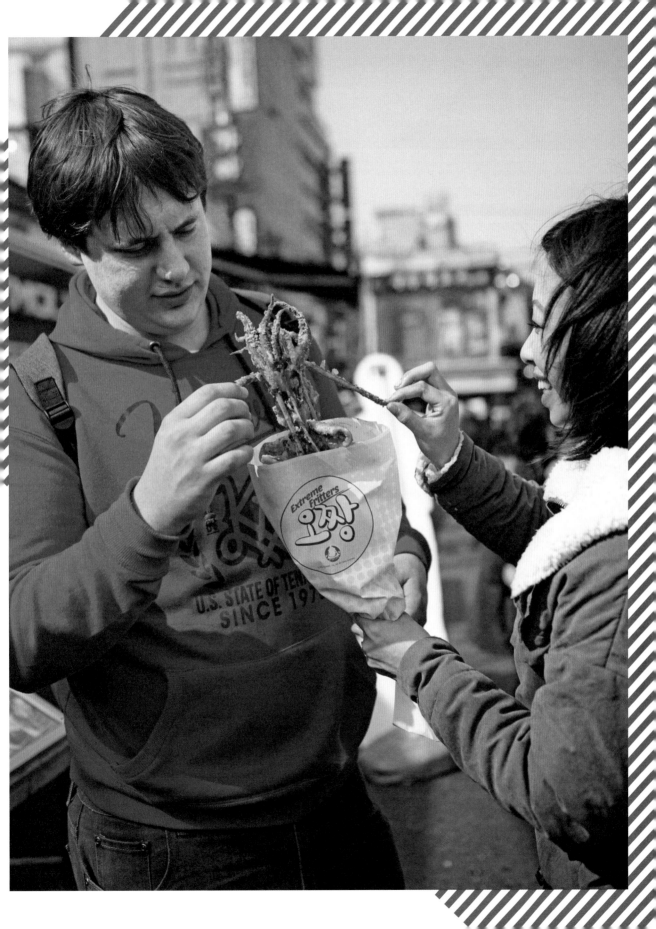

Spoon Pizza

Gareth and I had spoon pizza on our first trip to Korea together. We'd ordered it more out of curiosity than anything else at one of the pubs we visited with my cousin Jisoo. I can't remember what the toppings were on that first one we got, but the idea of eating pizza with a spoon stuck in our heads. Spoon pizza is about the best bit of the pizza – the cheesy, tomatoey, gooey topping – with the tortilla wrap acting simply as something for your spoon to scrape against as you dig into the pan. I can imagine lots of Italians looking at this recipe and shaking their heads in despair, but it really is the perfect sharing dish to be enjoyed with friends, armed with a few spoons and lots of drinks.

SERVES 4

2 flour tortilla wraps, cut into quarters
4 tablespoons *Gochujang* Ketchup (see page 80)
50g (1¾oz) medium Cheddar cheese, grated
50g (1¾oz) red Leicester cheese, grated

50g (1¾oz) soft mozzarella cheese
50g (1¾oz) *nduja* (hot Italian sausage paste)
2 tablespoons Really Great Cheese Sauce (see page 82)

1_ Preheat the oven to 200°C (400°F), Gas Mark 6.

2_ Lay half the tortilla quarters flat in a cast-iron griddle pan, with the curved edges on the outside to form a circle. Lay the remaining tortilla quarters over the top so that they overlap, ensuring the bottom of the pan is completely covered.

3_ Smear the *gochujang* ketchup all over the tortillas, making sure they are completely covered, then sprinkle over the grated cheeses. Tear the mozzarella into small pieces and dot over the surface of the pizza along with the *nduja*, then use a teaspoon to spoon small amounts of the cheese sauce all over.

4_ Put the pan in the oven and cook for 15 minutes, until all the cheese has completely melted and is gooey. Serve immediately – if you have a fondue set, place the pan on the stand over the flame to keep the cheese soft and melted.

TIP: The topping here can really be anything you like – I'm pretty sure we've had chicken and pepperoni on spoon pizzas before – so feel free to get creative and add any of your favourite pizza topping ingredients.

Gochu Twiguim CHEESY SPAM-STUFFED CHILLIES

Whenever I see any kind of stuffed, fried chilli on a menu, I have to have it — and if I ever saw this version on a menu, I'd be ordering it by the bucket-load. In Korea, fried chillies are both a common street food and *anju*, but they're usually filled with a *mandu*-style filling of minced pork. In this one, I've combined my love for the light, Korean-style batter, with my loves for cheese and Spam. The result is crispy, spicy chillies filled with oozy, melty cheese with a bit of meaty, salty bite from the Spam. Delicious.

MAKES 10

10 long green chillies
75g (2½oz) Spam, finely diced
½ onion, finely diced
½ bird's eye chilli, trimmed and finely sliced
250g (9oz) soft mozzarella cheese

vegetable oil, for frying
BATTER
150g (5½oz) plain flour
½ teaspoon baking powder
½ teaspoon garlic granules

½ teaspoon freshly ground black pepper
½ teaspoon salt
2 eggs

1_ For the batter, mix together the dry ingredients in a bowl. In a separate bowl, whisk together the eggs. Set aside.

2_ Using a sharp knife, make a cut down the middle of each long green chilli to create an opening, being careful not to go right through the other side. Remove the seeds and membranes.

3_ Heat a splash of vegetable oil in a frying pan over a medium heat, add the Spam, onion and bird's eye chilli and cook, stirring, for –5 minutes until the onions have softened and the Spam begins to brown and crisp at the edges.

4_ Tip the Spam, onion and chilli into a large bowl, tear over the mozzarella, add the salt and mix everything together with a wooden spoon. Spoon a tablespoon or so of the Spam and mozzarella mixture into each

chilli, being careful to fill them completely but not overstuff them. Press the chillies back together to seal the filling in.

5_ Half-fill a large pot or deep-fryer with vegetable oil and heat to 180°C (350°F), or until a cube of bread browns in 30 seconds.

6_ Dip a stuffed chilli into the beaten egg, moving it around with your fingertips to make sure it is fully coated, then dip it into the flour mix. Lightly toss the flour over the chilli to ensure it is fully coated on all sides, then carefully shake off any excess flour. Repeat with the remaining chillies.

7_ Lower the stuffed chillies carefully into the hot oil and fry for 2–3 minutes until golden. Remove from the fryer and shake off the excess oil, then leave to drain and cool for 2 minutes on kitchen paper before serving – be careful as they will be molten hot inside!

K-fries

Dripping in cheese, sour cream, *kimchi* and the meaty juices from the beef mince, Korean fries, or K-fries, are unapologetically messy. An American-Korean fusion food, they've been really big in the States (particularly L.A.) for quite some time now thanks to the likes of Roy Choi and his hugely popular Kogi taco trucks. They have also started to make their way over to Korea too and we've noticed several different variations of them on our last few visits. Just make sure you've got plenty of napkins before attempting to eat them!

SERVES 2

400g (14oz) oven French fries
vegetable oil, for frying
100g (3½oz) minced beef
50ml (2fl oz) *Bulgogi* Sauce (see page 95)
75g (2½oz) medium Cheddar cheese, grated
100g (3½oz) *Baechu Kimchi* (see page 32), drained and roughly chopped
1 long red pickled chilli, pickled overnight in Simple Pickle Brine (see page 82) and finely chopped
2 spring onions, trimmed and finely sliced, plus extra to garnish
2 tablespoons sour cream

1_ Cook the fries according to the packet instructions.

2_ Heat a splash of vegetable oil in a frying pan over a medium heat, add the minced beef and fry for 3–4 minutes until browned, then add the *bulgogi* sauce and cook for a further 2 minutes until the sauce has thickened and reduced. Set aside.

3_ Once cooked, remove the fries from the oven and place them in an ovenproof dish. Sprinkle a quarter of the cheese over the fries, then spoon the *bulgogi* beef mince over the top. Scatter over the *kimchi*, red chilli, spring onions and the rest of the cheese, then place the fries under a hot grill for 2 minutes, until the cheese is bubbling and melted.

4_ Dollop the sour cream generously over the fries, sprinkle with spring onions and serve immediately.

Gamja Hotdog CHIPS ON A STICK

These seem to be sold at almost every street food stall in Korea. Deep-fried hot-dogs coated in a cornmeal batter with fat chips stuck all over them, they look amazing, but the chips combined with the cornmeal batter often makes them quite stodgy. Still, we really wanted to bring a version back home as we thought that they had the potential to be great. After testing the recipe a few times, we discovered that straw fries were the way forward as they go really crispy in the fryer — giving you a crunchy outside with a soft cornmeal-battered hot-dog in the middle. Squeeze over lots of ketchup and American mustard for a truly authentic experience.

SERVES
4

4 baking potatoes, peeled
vegetable oil, for deep-frying
4 large hot-dogs

4 bamboo skewers, soaked in water for at least 10 minutes

BATTER
100g (3½oz) plain flour
100g (3½oz) cornmeal
2 teaspoons baking powder
1 tablespoon caster sugar
pinch of salt

150ml (¼ pint) milk
1 egg

TO SERVE
Gochujang Ketchup (see page 80)
American mustard

1_ Cut the potatoes into thin matchsticks using a sharp knife or a julienne peeler. Put the potato pieces in a colander and rinse under cold running water, then place in a large bowl with enough water to cover. Set aside for 10 minutes to draw out the excess starch.

2_ Meanwhile, put all the batter ingredients in a large bowl and mix together well. Set aside. Half-fill a large pot or deep-fryer with vegetable oil and heat to 180°C (350°F), or until a cube of bread browns in 30 seconds.

3_ Drain the potatoes and pat dry with kitchen paper, then lower them carefully into the hot oil. Fry for 10 seconds, then remove from the oil and drain on a tray lined with kitchen paper. Arrange the fries in an even layer, all roughly pointing in the same direction.

4_ Thread a bamboo skewer through the length of each hot-dog. Dip the hot-dog skewers in the batter one at a time, then spoon over extra batter to make sure they are completely coated. Lay one of the hot-dog skewers over the straw fries and gently roll it until coated all over, patting the fries into the batter. Repeat with the remaining skewers.

5_ Carefully lower the hot-dog skewers into the hot oil and fry for for 2–3 minutes, until the batter is crisp and golden brown. Drain on kitchen paper and serve with *gochujang* ketchup and American mustard.

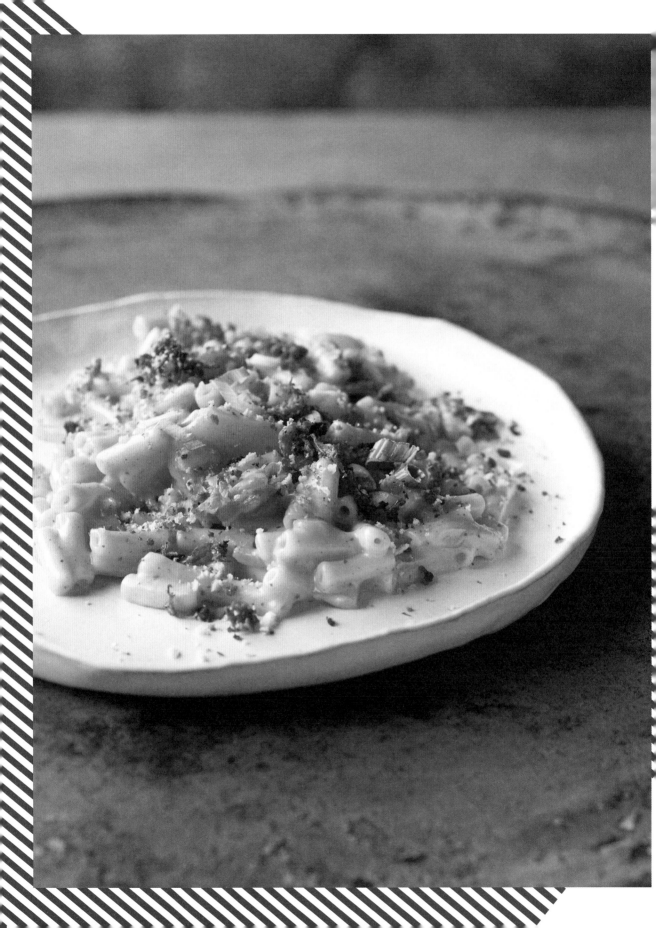

Kimchi Mac 'n' Cheese

There's something about *kimchi* and cheese together that just works — the tangy *kimchi* lifts the thick cheese sauce and gives it a bit of a chilli kick. Combined with the crunchy, salty breadcrumbs, this dish is pure comfort food. We've served this as a side dish at our pop-ups before, alongside our pork belly buns (see page 108), but this cheesy pasta is also great on its own.

SERVES 4

250g (9oz) Really Great Cheese Sauce (see page 82)
320g (11½oz) macaroni
2 tablespoons matured *Baechu Kimchi* (see page 32)
2 spring onions, trimmed and finely sliced

TOPPING
150g (5½oz) matured *Baechu Kimchi* (see page 32), drained and cut into 1-cm (½-inch) pieces
3 smoked streaky bacon rashers
½ tablespoon *gochugaru* (Korean red chilli powder)
1 small whole garlic clove
75g (2½oz) fresh breadcrumbs

1_ For the topping, lay the *kimchi* pieces flat on a large baking tray. Put in the oven on its lowest setting and leave for about 6 hours, or until dried out and crispy. Set aside.

2_ Put the bacon in a dry frying pan over a medium heat and fry for 3–4 minutes, until the edges start to go crispy and the bacon is cooked through. Tip into a blender along with the dried *kimchi*, *gochugaru* and garlic and pulse until everything is finely chopped. Return the pan to the heat, add the breadcrumbs and toast, stirring, for 4–5 minutes until the breadcrumbs are completely dry. Add to the other topping ingredients and set aside.

3_ Warm the cheese sauce over a moderate heat, stirring ocassionally and adding some extra milk if too thick. Set aside.

4_ Meanwhile, bring a pan of salted water to a boil, add the macaroni and cook according to the packet instructions until al dente. Drain and return to the pan, then mix in the cheese sauce, *kimchi* and spring onions. Spoon into bowls and scatter over a handful of the crispy topping to finish.

TIP: If you have one, place the *kimchi* topping pieces in a dehydrator rather than the oven to get them really dried out and crunchy.

Korean Fried Chicken

Double-fried, so the coating goes really crunchy but the meat stays juicy and really tender, Korean fried chicken really is the best kind of fried chicken there is. On a recent trip to Korea with some friends — and despite spending our days sampling all the street food that Korea has to offer, followed by evenings of Korean BBQ — we'd end our nights at a pub with a big plateful of the stuff. Well, you have to order *anju* in a pub and the chicken was always too hard to resist, no matter how full we were. Nothing goes better with an ice-cold beer.

SERVES 4

1kg (2lb 4oz) chicken wings
1 litre (1¾ pints) *Kimchi* Brine (see page 94)
vegetable oil, for deep-frying
3 eggs
½ quantity Korean Sweet Chilli Sauce (see page 86),
    for brushing

COATING
180g (6oz) potato starch
60g (2¼oz) sweet rice flour
80g (3oz) self-raising flour
1 tablespoon baking powder
½ tablespoon salt

1_ Put the chicken wings in a large bowl and pour over the brine. Transfer to the refrigerator and leave to brine for 1 hour.

2_ After 1 hour, drain the chicken wings and rinse them under cold running water to remove the excess salt from the brine, then pat dry with kitchen paper.

3_ Half-fill a large pot or deep-fryer with vegetable oil and heat to 180°C (350°F), or until a cube of bread browns in 30 seconds.

4_ Put the chicken in a large bowl. Crack the eggs over the top and rub in using your hands. In a separate bowl, mix together the coating ingredients. Tip the mix over the chicken and massage with your hands until evenly coated.

5_ Shake the chicken wings gently to remove any excess coating, then carefully lower into the hot oil. Fry for 4–5 minutes until the chicken begins to colour.

6_ Lift the chicken out of the oil for 4–5 minutes (this will allow the oil to get back up to temperature as well as allow the chicken a moment to rest), then carefully lower the chicken back into the oil and fry for a further 3 minutes until golden.

7_ Drain the chicken on kitchen paper, brush with a little chilli sauce and serve immediately with plenty of napkins.

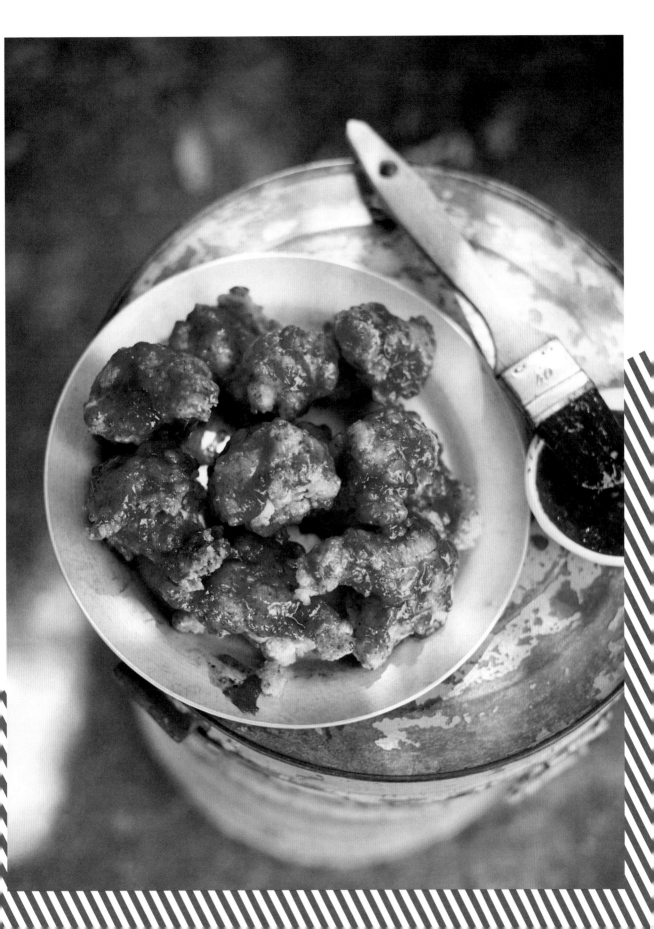

Garlicky Gizzards

I don't know many people who ate chickens' gizzards growing up, but I've always been a fan. We spent quite a lot of summer holidays in Spain, and my mum would often pick up a pack of chickens' gizzards from the local supermarket. She'd bring them back to the house and quickly sauté them with fresh chilli, garlic and salt. Cooked quickly like this, the gizzards are quite chewy (which I like), but Gareth has never been too convinced of the texture, so we found that brining the gizzards first and trimming them of any sinew makes them much more tender, while still retaining their flavour. We've added a little bit of chickens' liver here too to balance out the texture.

SERVES 2

200g (7oz) chickens' gizzards, cleaned and trimmed of any sinew
1 litre (1¾pints) *Kimchi* Brine (see page 94)
1½ tablespoons vegetable oil

50g (1¾oz) chickens' livers, cleaned, trimmed of any sinew and cut into thin strips
1 teaspoon salted butter
1 long red chilli, trimmed, deseeded and finely sliced

2 garlic cloves, finely sliced
pinch of salt
pinch of pepper
1 tablespoon *soju* (Korean rice/grain spirit) or sake
½ spring onion, trimmed and finely sliced, to garnish

1_ Put the gizzards in a large bowl and pour over the brine. Transfer to the refrigerator and leave to brine for 1 hour.

2_ After 1 hour, drain the gizzards and rinse them under cold running water to remove the excess salt from the brine, then pat dry with kitchen paper.

3_ Heat 1 tablespoon of the vegetable oil in a large frying pan over a high heat. Add the livers and fry, stirring, for 30 seconds, then add ½ teaspoon of butter to the pan. Once the butter has melted, tip the livers into a bowl and set to one side.

4_ Return the pan to the heat and add the remaining ½ tablespoon of oil. Reduce the heat to medium, add the gizzards, chilli, garlic, salt and pepper and fry for 2–3 minutes until the gizzards are cooked through. Add the *soju*, livers and remaining butter to the frying pan and fry a further 30 seconds. Transfer to a plate and serve garnished with the spring onion.

TIP: These gizzards also make a great starter. Toast a couple of slices of rye or sourdough bread in the frying pan after cooking to soak up the juices, then spoon over the gizzard mix to finish.

Chorizo and Kimchi Hash

With its winning combination of smoky chorizo, tangy *kimchi* and runny eggs, this hash is the ultimate brunch food — although it's just as good shared as an *anju* to help soak up all that beer.

SERVES 2

500g (1lb 2oz) new potatoes
1 tablespoon vegetable oil
1 red onion, finely sliced
50g (1¾oz) dried chorizo sausage, finely chopped
100g *Baechu Kimchi* (see page 32), drained

5 cherry tomatoes, halved
1 garlic clove, minced
2 eggs
salt
buttered crusty bread slices, to serve

TO GARNISH
1 spring onion, trimmed and finely chopped
1 teaspoon *gochugaru* (Korean red chilli powder)

1_ Bring a large saucepan of salted water to the boil, add the potatoes and cook for 15 minutes, until tender. Drain and rinse under cold water and cut into bite-sized chunks.

2_ Heat the oil in a cast-iron griddle pan. Fry the onion and chorizo for 2–3 minutes, until the onion has just softened. Add the *kimchi*, tomatoes and garlic and fry for a further minute, then add the potatoes and cook, stirring gently, for a further 2 minutes.

3_ Make two wells in the centre of the hash with a spoon and crack an egg into each. Put the pan under a hot grill for 3–4 minutes, until the whites of the eggs are cooked through but the yolks are still runny.

4_ Garnish with spring onion and *gochugaru* and serve immediately with thick slices of crusty buttered bread.

Lotus Root Nachos

Sweet, salty and moreish, these crispy nachos are a twist on the traditional and make for the perfect party snack. They require minimum effort, while the pretty pattern of the sliced lotus roots looks seriously impressive. Lotus roots are traditionally served as *banchan*, often braised in soy sauce. Though they look attractive, I never think that they taste that great, and I much prefer eating them like this.

SERVES 4

4 lotus roots, about 200g (7oz) each, trimmed
juice of 1 lemon
vegetable oil, for deep-frying

SEASONING
1 teaspoon salt

1 teaspoon sesame oil
1 tablespoon garlic granules
1½ teaspoons caster sugar
1 tablespoon *gochugaru* (Korean red chilli powder)
1 tablespoon paprika

TO SERVE
Zingy Green Sauce (see page 79)
Kimchi Salsa (see page 79)

1_ Using a sharp knife or a mandoline, cut the lotus root widthways into 3-mm (⅛-inch) slices. Place the lotus root slices in a bowl, covering them with the lemon juice as you go to prevent them from turning brown.

2_ Half-fill a large pot or deep-fryer with vegetable oil and heat to 180°C (350°F), or until a cube of bread browns in 30 seconds. Lower the lotus root slices carefully into the hot oil a few at a time (to prevent them sticking to each other) and fry for 3 minutes, until the slices are crisp and slightly browned. Shake off any excess oil and leave to drain on kitchen paper while repeating with the remaining slices.

3_ Meanwhile, mix together all the seasoning ingredients in a small bowl. Tip the lotus root slices into a large bowl and sprinkle over the seasoning mixture a pinch at a time to prevent the seasoning powder from clumping together. Toss the lotus root slices until they are thoroughly coated, then serve with zingy green sauce and *kimchi* salsa.

10

Sweet Treats

A SHIP WILL GO TO THE MOUNTAIN
IF THERE ARE TOO MANY CAPTAINS

Traditionally, Korea's never had that much in the way of desserts. As Korean food is served all at the same time rather than as different courses, Korean restaurants rarely have any sort of dessert offering and instead fruit is usually eaten at the end of the meal.

There are a couple of sweet treats that are famous in Korea such as *hotteok*, the chewy, crispy pancakes filled with caramel, and *bingsu*, a snowy, shaved ice that's eaten in the summer, but even these aren't usually eaten at the end the meal. *Hotteok* is a popular street food and *bingsu* is usually sold in cafes, separate from where you'd eat your main meal.

Even for special occasions, when sweet treats do sometimes make an appearance, the treats are usually in the form of biscuits or rice cakes called *tteok*. *Tteok* are a chewier, stickier version of the Japanese *mochi* rice cakes, and are often shaped into half-moon shaped sweets called *songpyeon*. These are often filled with sweetened red bean paste or sugar and sesame seeds and are usually eaten during *Chusok* (Korean Thanksgiving).

Rice cakes don't really feel like a dessert to me though, and because desserts aren't really a big thing in Korea, we've always come up with Western-style desserts that incorporate Korean flavours for our pop-ups and events. These include our *Yuja* Cheesecake (see page 220) and our Blueberry *Mandu* (see page 227), which is a little twist on the sweet Polish *pierogi* dumpling.

Korea does have a lot of bakeries though – in fact, in the bigger cities such as Seoul and Busan, it's difficult to walk down a street without passing one. These bakeries are often big chains which all sell similar breads and cakes. Some of the offerings are often a little unusual (think hot-dog doughnuts, or tuna sandwiches on sugary, sweet bread), whereas others are more typically cake-like, such as *Soborro*, a peanutty crumble bread that we've based our cake recipe on (see page 224).

I think that a lot of the reasons why people like certain desserts are due to nostalgia – it's probably why I like *Soborro* so much, because it's my go-to whenever I visit a Korean bakery. It's also the reason that we had to include a recipe for banana milk here. You might say that banana milk isn't much of a dessert, but our version is thick, creamy and full of ice cream, so it makes a great end to a meal.

Yuja Cheesecake

For our first pop-up, we had to think really hard about a suitable dessert, as Korea isn't particularly known for its sweet treats. After playing around with a few ideas, we decided on this *yuja* cheesecake. *Yuja* is the Korean word for yuzu, a citrus fruit that has the zesty freshness of a lemon but with a slightly bitter edge. Here it combines perfectly with the rich cream cheese, to create a tangy, sweet dessert.

SERVES 8–10

200ml (7fl oz) double cream
300g (10½oz) cream cheese
100g (3½oz) golden caster sugar
4 tablespoons *yuja* (yuzu) juice

BASE
90g (3¼oz) gingernut biscuits
60g (2¼oz) digestive biscuits
75g (2½oz) salted butter, melted

JELLY
200g (7oz) *Yuja* Curd (see page 222)
2 tablespoons *yuja* (yuzu) juice
½ teaspoon gelatine powder

1_ For the base, break the biscuits into a food processor and blend to a fine powder. Add the melted butter and stir together until the mixture resembles wet sand.

2_ Spread the biscuit mix over the base of a loose-bottomed 20-cm (8-inch) round cake tin, pressing it down with the back of a spoon to create an even layer. Transfer to the freezer for 5 minutes to set.

3_ Meanwhile, pour the double cream into a mixing bowl and whisk to form stiff peaks. Add the cream cheese, sugar and *yuja* juice and beat everything together.

4_ Remove the tin from the freezer and spread the cream cheese mixture evenly over the biscuit base. Transfer to the refrigerator and leave to chill and set for at least 4 hours.

5_ Once set, make the jelly. Gently heat the *yuja* curd and juice in a small saucepan over a medium heat, being careful not to let the mixture boil. Once hot, add the gelatine powder and stir continuously over the heat for 10–12 minutes, until all the gelatine has dissolved into the liquid. Remove from the heat and leave to cool to room temperature.

6_ Remove the cheesecake from the refrigerator and pour the jelly mixture evenly over the top. Return to the refrigerator and leave to set overnight before serving the following day.

Yuja Curd

This zesty, tangy, sweet curd has so many uses. Lemon curd has always been one of my favourite toast toppings, but *yuja* curd feels more like a special treat. Stir it into yogurt for breakfast, use it as a topping on desserts or simply spread it on toast for a simple, delicious and easy snack.

MAKES
1
SMALL JAR

2 eggs, plus 2 extra yolks
100g (3½oz) butter
200g (7oz) caster sugar

6 tablespoons *yuja* (yuzu) juice
zest of 2 lemons

1_ Lightly whisk the whole eggs and egg yolks together in a bowl.

2_ Melt the butter in a saucepan over a medium heat. Once liquid, add the sugar and mix together with a wooden spoon. Stir in the *yuja* juice and lemon zest, then add the eggs and continue to cook, stirring, for 8–10 minutes, until the mixture is creamy and thick enough to coat the back of a spoon.

3_ Remove the pan from the heat and leave the curd to cool, then pour into a sterilized jar and seal. Keep in the refrigerator until ready to use. This will keep for up to a month unopened but use within a week once the jar is opened.

Bingsu SUMMER SNOW

There is nothing better than *bingsu* in the summer. Made from shaved or crushed frozen milk, it cools you down much faster than eating ice cream and it's so light and refreshing. *Bingsu* can be topped with any fruit you like – on our most recent trip to Korea, I got hooked on a 'mango cheese' version, which sounds weird, but essentially tasted like a mango cheesecake ice cream. Tinned fruit works well here, as the fruit is always soft enough to break apart with your spoon.

SERVES 4

600ml (20fl oz) milk
1 x 425g (15oz) tin mango slices, drained
vanilla ice cream, to serve

'CHEESECAKE' MIX
3 tablespoons cream cheese
4 tablespoons double cream
2 tablespoons caster sugar

1_ Pour the milk into ice cube trays and place them in the freezer for 3–4 hours, until just set. (Don't allow the ice cubes to set too solid, as they will not break down properly in the food processor if you do.)

2_ Meanwhile, mix together all the 'cheesecake' ingredients in a small bowl. Set aside.

3_ Once the milky ice cubes have just frozen, tip them into a food processor and pulse briefly together until the icy mixture resembles snow (it shouldn't become too wet like a slushie).

4_ Pour the ice mixture into a large bowl, then pile over the mango slices. Using a teaspoon, dot little lumps of the 'cheesecake' mix all over the *bingsu* and serve with a generous scoop of vanilla ice cream in the middle.

TIP: Nowadays in Korea, *bingsu* often comes with a side of condensed milk, which you pour all over the top to make things really creamy and to add a little more sweetness. If you've got a sweet tooth, give it a try.

Soborro Cake

In Korea, *soborro* is actually a non-sweet bread, and one that I only really enjoy for its peanut butter crumble topping – I love to peel off all the crumble bits and eat them like little biscuits. Here we've sweetened things up a bit, giving it a peanut butter sponge base and a buttercream filling to go with all those delicious peanut buttery crumble bits. It's sweet with a slightly salty edge, and goes perfectly with a coffee.

SERVES
8-10

175g (6oz) softened unsalted butter, plus extra for
   greasing
200g (7oz) caster sugar
3 eggs
4 tablespoons crunchy peanut butter
25g (1oz) roasted, salted peanuts
200g (7oz) self-raising flour
1 teaspoon baking powder

TOPPING
60g (2¼oz) plain flour
40g (1½oz) caster sugar
40g (1½oz) cold butter, cut into cubes
1½ tablespoons crunchy peanut butter
10g (¼oz) roasted, salted peanuts

FILLING
70g (2½oz) unsalted butter, cut into cubes
1½ tablespoons crunchy peanut butter
15g (½oz) icing sugar
pinch of salt
1 tablespoon milk

1_ Grease a 20-cm (8-inch) loose-bottomed round cake tin with a little butter and line the base with nonstick baking paper. Preheat the oven to 180°C (350°F), Gas Mark 4.

2_ For the topping, put all the ingredients in a large bowl and rub the mixture between your fingertips until it resembles coarse breadcrumbs. Set aside.

3_ In a large bowl, cream together the butter and sugar until pale and fluffy. Stir in the eggs, peanut butter and peanuts and beat together until the peanut butter is no longer in lumps and everything is mixed together well. Slowly add the flour and baking powder to the bowl and stir everything together to form a smooth cake batter.

4_ Spoon the batter into the prepared cake tin, smoothing out the top with the base of a spoon so that it is even. Sprinkle over the crumble topping evenly and bake for 45 minutes, or until a metal skewer inserted into the middle of the cake comes out clean.

5_ Meanwhile, put all the filling ingredients in a large
bowl and mix together well until smooth and creamy.
Set aside.

6_ Once the cake is cooked, remove from the tin and
leave to cool completely on a wire rack. Once cooled,
slice the cake in half horizontally. Carefully remove
the top half and put to one side, then smear the
peanut butter filling generously over the bottom half of
the cake. Sandwich the cake halves back together
and serve.

Blueberry Mandu

A cross between Korean *mandu* and Polish *pierogi*, these crispy dumplings are filled with sweet blueberries and smell like pancakes as they crisp up in the frying pan. I'd never considered eating *mandu* as a dessert before — I've definitely never seen them in Korea — but my friend Magda introduced me to Polish *pierogis* and put the idea in my head. With traditional *mandu* dumplings, we would usually fold the tops to make pretty parcels, which half-fry and half-steam, but with these it's better to crimp the edges with a fork, so that the dumplings can lay flatter in the frying pan and get really crispy on both sides.

SERVES
2

1 tablespoon plain flour
2 tablespoons caster sugar
pinch of salt
120g (4½oz) blueberries

8 large *mandu* skins, either shop-bought or homemade
(see page 24)
2 tablespoons vegetable oil

TO SERVE
Yuja Curd (see page 222)
vanilla ice cream

1_ Combine the flour, sugar and salt in a mixing bowl. Add the blueberries, gently crushing half of them with the back of a fork as you go. Mix everything together thoroughly to form a paste. Set aside.

2_ Fill a small bowl with a little cold water.

3_ Lay a *mandu* skin flat in the palm of your hand, and spoon 1 teaspoon of the blueberry mix into the centre. Dip the thumb and forefinger of your free hand into the water and use them to fold over one side of the skin to form a semicircular parcel. Seal the

mandu together by lightly pressing the edges with the tines of a fork, ensuring there are no gaps. Repeat with the remaining *mandu* skins and filling.

4_ Heat the oil in a large frying pan over a medium-high heat. Add the *mandu* and fry for at least 30 seconds on each side, until lightly browned and crisp (homemade dumpling skins will take slightly longer). Drain the *mandu* on kitchen paper and serve with vanilla ice cream and a tablespoon of *yuja* curd.

Hotteok SALTED CARAMEL-FILLED PANCAKES

Hotteok are traditionally sold as street food and can be found all over Korea. They're a chewy cross between a doughnut and a pancake, filled with a cinnamon sugar that melts to become a caramel as they fry. In Busan (where you can find the best *hotteok*), they add nuts and seeds too, and that's my favourite way to eat them. For the sugar filling to be completely melted they have to be served hot, but be careful as the inside can become molten. It's said that *hotteok* get their name from the 'ho' noise made from blowing on them to cool them down — don't forget to do this before taking your first bite!

MAKES
8
PANCAKES

1 teaspoon active dried yeast
1½ tablespoons caster sugar
5 tablespoons warm water
6 tablespoons warm milk, plus extra if needed
200g (7oz) plain flour, plus extra for dusting

50g (1¾oz) sweet rice flour
1 teaspoon vegetable oil, plus extra for frying
generous knob of butter

FILLING
2 tablespoons ground hazelnuts

2 tablespoons pine nuts
150g (5½oz) tablespoons soft dark brown sugar
25g (1oz) roasted, salted peanuts, crushed
pinch of ground cinnamon
pinch of salt

1_ For the filling, mix together the ingredients in a small bowl. Set aside.

2_ In a separate small bowl, mix together the yeast, sugar, water and milk. Set aside for 10 minutes to allow the yeast to activate.

3_ In a large bowl, mix together the flour and sweet rice flour. Slowly add the milky yeast mixture to the bowl, stirring together with a wooden spoon to form a dough.

4_ Tip the dough out onto a lightly floured surface and knead for 10 minutes until smooth and elastic, adding a few extra drops of milk if the dough is still feeling a little dry. Put the dough in a mixing bowl and brush lightly with the vegetable oil. Cover loosely with clingfilm and leave in a warm place for 45 minutes, or until doubled in size.

5_ Gently tip the risen dough out onto a lightly floured surface and knead for a further 2–3 minutes to loosen it up again. Divide the dough into eight equal-sized pieces and form into little balls. For each ball, flatten it out in your hand, to form a round disc, approximately 1cm (½ inch) thick.

6_ Using the heel of your hand create a well in the centre of each dough disc. Spoon 1–1½ tablespoons of the sugar filling evenly over the centre of each disc, then fold the edges into the centre to seal in the filling. Gently flatten the dough again to form a 1-cm (½-inch) thick pancake.

7_ Heat the butter and a splash of oil in a heavy-based frying pan, over a medium heat. Fry the pancakes one at a time for 1–2 minutes on each side, until crispy and golden brown. Drain on kitchen paper and serve immediately.

TIP: Heat any leftover sugar mix with a little water to create a caramel which you can spoon on top of the *hotteok* and ice cream.

My Mum's Miracle Cure

For as long as I can remember, this has been my family's go-to recipe for whenever anyone comes down with a cold. Its fresh, citrussy taste is quite strong — I used to hate it as a kid, though I've grown to like it as I've gotten older. I swear it'll get rid of a cold within 24 hours.

MAKES
2-3
MUGS

2 pears, halved
2 large oranges, quartered
1 lemon, quartered
1 lime, halved

100g (3½oz) fresh root ginger, roughly chopped
1 litre (1¾ pints) water
clear runny honey, to serve

1_ Put all the ingredients in a large saucepan over a high heat. Bring to the boil, reduce to a simmer and leave to cook, uncovered, for 25 minutes until reduced by about half.

2_ Remove from the heat and leave to cool slightly, then ladle the liquid into mugs. Stir in a teaspoon or so of honey to sweeten. Drink up.

> **TIP:** You can adapt this recipe to your own taste — my mum's recipe is an adaptation of my grandmother's, and mine is an adaptation of my mum's. The key ingredients are whole, large oranges for vitamin C and pears to soothe a sore throat; the rest is up to you.

Ba-na-na Oo-You BANANA MILK

Whenever we visited my grandparents in Busan we'd take them a bag of their favourite treats, which would almost always include little bottles of banana milk. Bananas used to be really expensive in Korea, so when banana milk was introduced into the country it quickly became a big hit with both young and old. While I never really drink it in England, as I'm not a huge fan of its artificial sweetness, I still always pick up a bottle when I'm in Korea as it brings back such childhood memories. This recipe is for the ultimate banana milk — an American-style, thick ice cream shake with lots of banana flavour. Perfectly ice cold, sweet but not sickly, it's just really, really great.

MAKES
1
GLASS

1 ripe banana
5 ice cubes
1 tablespoon malted drink powder (such as Ovaltine)

½ tablespoon soft brown sugar
2 tablespoons vanilla ice cream
150ml (¼ pint) semi-skimmed milk

1_ Peel and roughly chop the banana. Wrap the banana pieces in clingfilm and freeze for 1–2 hours, or until needed.

2_ Put the frozen banana pieces in a blender with all the other ingredients. Blend together until smooth, then pour into a tall glass. Serve with a thick straw.

Busan BBQ

Since starting Busan BBQ in August 2012, it's been a bit of an adventure. We probably would have planned things a little differently if we had had more time, but we really wanted to get up and running for that summer.

Though it all started with a *Bulgogi* Burger, we felt like we needed to add a few other items to our menu before we started trading. We originally spent quite a lot of time working on the *Bulgogi* Burger recipe, but the ideas for the Pork Belly Bun and Korean Fried Chicken came pretty easily. Gareth was insistent that we include Korean Fried Chicken on the menu as it's one of his favourite things to eat, and we decided that three options would be good to start with in order to offer variety without stretching ourselves too thinly. Though we've tweaked our recipes a little since we started, these three are still the regulars on our menu.

We traded at our first market in North Finchley at (the now closed) North London Artisan Market. It was an early start as our trailer was kept a two-hour drive from our house (which was also a three-hour drive to North Finchley) and we had to be at the market for 8.30am. It was a grey, rainy day and we were both tired from the long drive and early start. We'd thought we had enough time to get ourselves sorted when we arrived, but on that first day we still had all our kitchen equipment in its original boxes so we didn't know where anything was and we also hadn't prepared any marinades, sauces or burgers, with the intention of doing it all when we arrived. Looking back, I'm not quite sure why we thought that was even possible. Our power kept flickering on and off and we were so behind and running around like headless chickens. Fortunately, we were lucky enough to trade at that first market with Nisha and Nishma from Grill My Cheese and Emily from Rupert Street who gave us so much help and advice on the day and we've stayed good friends with them since. From that first experience, we certainly learnt that being prepped for a market is really important.

We'd hoped to join the guys at Street Feast ever since we started trading. Street Feast are the biggest night (though they now include lunch) markets in London, with a strong emphasis on the best traders, food and vibes. We were lucky because Adam from

Street Feast visited us one day and tried our *Bulgogi* Burger. We were so nervous but a couple of days later he invited us to trade at the opening weekend of Street Feast that summer. To this day, that first day at Street Feast was probably the biggest highlight of our time trading. It was busy on completely another level, despite the fact that the weather was awful. People still queued and were amazingly patient, all having a great time huddled under umbrellas.

We've traded at Street Feast ever since. Street Feast makes sure all their traders are always thinking about developing their food and making progress. They've definitely pushed us to be at our best and to challenge ourselves and we're thankful for that.

Apart from markets, we've also held a number of pop ups in restaurants and bars such as a month at Gordon Ramsay's Bread Street Kitchen for a Korean themed bar. Pop ups give us the opportunity to be more creative with our dishes and experiment, as we're usually in a full size kitchen.

There's nothing like working in street food though – you have the chance to really interact with the customer. You get to watch as they take away their burger or fried chicken and take that first bite; when they close their eyes and start nodding, you know you've done something right. And the best part is when we see people recommending us to their friends. The fact that someone's enjoyed our food so much, they want their friends to love it as much as they do feels amazing. Seeing someone point at our trailer and hear them saying, 'You have to try the burger from those guys, it's so good,' makes the long hours and hard work definitely feel like it's completely worth it.

Suppliers

Seoul Plaza stores
www.koreafoods.co.uk
36 High Street
New Malden KT3 4HE
Tel: 020 8949 4329

91–93 Mill Road
Cambridge CB1 2AW
Tel: 01223 303 610

136 Golders Green Road
London NW11 8HB
Tel: 020 8731 7999

336 Wimborne Road
Winton
Bournemouth BH9 2HH
Tel: 01202 527 177

The Brook
536 Bristol Road
Birmingham B29 6BD
Tel: 0121 472 2331

Reading University Students' Union
University of Reading, Whiteknights
Reading RG6 6UQ
Tel: 0118 986 1025

Unit 13/14
Cannon Park Shopping Centre
Coventry CV4 7EH
Tel: 02476 693 862

Asia Market
www.asiamarket.ie
Merrywell Business Park
Ballymount Road Lower, Ballymount
Dublin 12 D12 W327
Tel: +353 1 409 7072

Asia Supermarket Belfast
www.asiabelfast.com
189 Ormeau Road
Belfast BT7 1SQ
Tel: 028 90 326396

BHL Oriental Food Store
www.bhloriental.co.uk
1–4 King William Street
Exeter EX4 6PD
Tel: 01392 759 391

Hang Won Hong
www.hangwonhong.com
Connaught Building, 58–60 George Street
Manchester M1 4HF
Tel: 0161 228 6182

HiYoU Supermarket
www.hiyou.eu
108 Newgate Street
Newcastle upon Tyne NE1 5RQ
Tel: 0191 232 2311

Korea Foods Mart
www.koreafoods.co.uk
Unit 5 Wyvern Industrial Estate
Beverley Way, New Malden KT3 4PH
Tel: 020 8949 2238

Matthews Foods Ltd
www.matthewsfoods.co.uk
Unit 1, Barrat Trading Estate
230–260 Garscube Road
Glasgow G4 9RR
Tel: 0141 332 1688

136–138 Causewayend
Aberdeen AB25 3TN
Tel: 01224 636 060

Oriental Mart (UK) Ltd
www.orientalmart.co.uk
6–8 Heathcoat Street
Nottingham NG1 3AA
Tel: 0115 950 6615

Oriental Supermarket Birmingham Ltd
www.orientalsuper.com
100 Holloway Head
Birmingham B1 1NB
Tel: 0121 666 6131

SK Mart
www.skmart.co.uk
17 Goldhurst Terrace
London NW6 3HX
Tel: 020 7625 6800

Speciality Cooking Supplies Ltd
www.souschef.co.uk
Tel: 0800 270 7591
Online Only

Tai Fat Supermarket
5 Melton St
Leicester LE1 3NB
Tel: 0116 262 9656

Tai Sun Oriental
www.taisun-group.co.uk
17–19, Matilda Street
Sheffield S1 4QB
Tel: 01114 278 6068

Wai Yee Hong
www.waiyeehong.com
Eastgate Oriental City
Eastgate Road, Eastville
Bristol BS5 6XX
Tel: 0117 952 4240

Sing Kee Foods
www.singkeefoods.co.uk
Sing-Kee Building
30–36 Cross Stamford Street
Leeds LS7 1BA
Tel: 0113 2468 838

35–39 North Parade
Bradford BD1 3JH
Tel: 01274 304 288

Index

Acknowledgements

We have a lot of people to thank for helping us with both Busan BBQ and for this book, so please forgive us if we've left any names out – and be prepared for a long list!

Firstly, thank you to Cindy for giving us a chance at our first trading opportunity at North London Artisan Market and really believing in our food! Similarly, thanks to The Cheesers – Nisha and Nishma from Grill My Cheese – you made our first day trading all the easier by filling it with lots of laughs among the chaos.

Richard, Riv, Dave, Cecile, Alex, Abbie, Moses and Gareth (the other one), thank you for helping us out in those times that we've needed an extra pair of hands... and to Jack for being our most enthusiastic and dedicated customer.

Shaun Searley, Allan Pickett, Neil Rankin – your advice and expertise over the past couple of years has really helped improve and develop our recipes as well as filling our heads with lots of ideas.

Adam, JD and the team at Street Feast/London Union – being part of Street Feast has pushed us to be a better business and to constantly evolve in the competitive world of street food. We're so thankful for the opportunities you've given us and look forward to growing with you and London Union.

Andre from Bluebird, Damon, Dan at Korea Foods and the boys from the Quality Chop – thanks for keeping us stocked with supplies. You're the best suppliers we could ask for.

Mrs. Kim at Korea Foods, thank you for taking me under your wing. I'm not sure you've ever realised how much wisdom and knowledge you imparted to me – your enthusiasm for cooking delicious Korean meals is really inspiring.

The look for Busan BBQ would have been very different without the help from the creative geniuses at Colt – particularly Alex and John. Thank you for helping us shape our vague ideas into a strong brand identity.

To everyone that's eaten from us – your support means that we're able to work in a job we love.

Anna at Johnson & Alcock – thank you for getting in touch and encouraging us to write this book. I don't think we would have dreamed that it'd be possible, but you've been so supportive and helpful in making this into a reality.

Denise, Yasia, Pauline and the team at Octopus – we're so proud that this book has turned out the way we'd hoped. Actually – even better than we could have hoped, so thank you for your never ending patience and for really listening to us.

Thanks to David and Victoria for creating such beautiful pictures and for Annie and Lola for making our food look so delicious. We hope the kimchi fried rice has become a favourite weekday dinner!

And to the final thank you... to Umma and Dad – for your never ending support, advice, love, wisdom and everything else – none of this would have been possible without you.

For Noah, our little one – and also for Gareth. Without your help in testing the recipes, your comprehensive note-taking, tasting (eating) all the dishes, and – most importantly – your never-ending patience and support, this book couldn't have happened. Love you both to the moon and back.

An Hachette UK Company
www.hachette.co.uk

First published in Great Britain in 2016 by Mitchell Beazley, a division of Octopus Publishing Group Ltd
Carmelite House
50 Victoria Embankment
London EC4Y 0DZ
www.octopusbooks.co.uk

This material was previously published as *K Food* in 2016

First published in paperback in 2018

ISBN 978-1-78472-479-5

A CIP catalogue record for this book is available from the British Library.

Printed and bound in China

10 9 8 7 6 5 4 3

Group publishing director: Denise Bates
Editor: Pauline Bache
Art director: Yasia Williams
Food photograher: David Munns
Location photographer in Korea: Ben Weller
Home economist: Annie Rigg
Props stylist: Victoria Allen
Designed by Grade Design
Assistant production manager: Caroline Alberti

Standard level spoon measurements are used in all recipes.
1 tablespoon = one 15 ml spoon
1 teaspoon = one 5 ml spoon

Both imperial and metric measurements have been given in all recipes. Use one set of measurements only and not a mixture of both.

Eggs should be medium unless otherwise stated. The Department of Health advises that eggs should not be consumed raw. This book contains dishes made with raw or lightly cooked eggs. It is prudent for more vulnerable people such as pregnant and nursing mothers, invalids, the elderly, babies and young children to avoid uncooked or lightly cooked dishes made with eggs. Once prepared these dishes should be kept refrigerated and used promptly.

Milk should be full fat unless otherwise stated.

Fresh herbs should be used unless otherwise stated. If unavailable use dried herbs as an alternative but halve the quantities stated.

Ovens should be preheated to the specific temperature – if using a fan-assisted oven, follow manufacturer's instructions for adjusting the time and the temperature.

Pepper should be freshly ground black pepper unless otherwise stated.

This book includes dishes made with nuts and nut derivatives. It is advisable for customers with known allergic reactions to nuts and nut derivatives and those who may be potentially vulnerable to these allergies, such as pregnant and nursing mothers, invalids, the elderly, babies and children, to avoid dishes made with nuts and nut oils. It is also prudent to check the labels of pre-prepared ingredients for the possible inclusion of nut derivatives.

Vegetarians should look for the 'V' symbol on a cheese to ensure it is made with vegetarian rennet. There are vegetarian forms of Parmesan, feta, Cheddar, Cheshire, Red Leicester, dolcelatte and many goats' cheeses, among others.